TAJ MAHAL SHRINE OF LIES

IZ

Copyright © 2023 by IZ

All rights reserved.

This book or any portion thereof may not be reproduced or used in any manner whatsoever without the express written permission of the respective writer of the respective content except for the use of brief quotations in a book review.

The writer of the respective work holds sole responsibility for the originality of the content and The Write Order is not responsible in any way whatsoever.

Disclaimer: The publishers do not share the views conveyed in this book and are not responsible for the opinions of the author. This stands good even for the opinions expressed of the characters in the book.

Printed in India

ISBN: 978-93-95868-15-0

First Printing, 2023

The Write Order

Koramangala, Bangalore

Karnataka-560029

THE WRITE ORDER PUBLICATIONS.

www.thewriteorder.com

Book Cover Designed by Sankhoshubro Nath

"Rather than love, than money, than fame, give me truth."

-Henry David Thoreau

NOTE FROM THE AUTHOR

THIS BOOK IS OPEN TO CRITICISM.

IZ has written this book from the perspective of a young man.

The author has used the term Mughal Emperor only to refer to the Emperors of India. The term "Mughal(s)" or "Mughal Emperor(s)" should not be viewed/considered in any way or by any means as a reference to the Muslim Community of the present day.

The author doesn't believe in any religion and his views on all religions are neutral. No religion, community or individual (except for the one mentioned in the book who is already dead centuries ago) is being targeted through this book. Author's views regarding God are neutral as he neither denies nor accepts the existence of God. Even if God exists, the author has a different approach to the existence of God. The author puts himself under the category of agnostics, freethinkers, atheists, or many terms like these because the author doesn't have a single word or definition that would suffice to portray the beliefs and ideologies of the author's intellect.

The author is just targeting a barbaric despot who has done much wrong to the people. The author is well aware of all the incidents of communal hate mongering and religious extremism happening in India for the past few years. To be frank, India has always been polarised on the basis of religion for centuries. This book hasn't been written to spread hate and propaganda, but rather, to tell the truth about a monstrous autarch and his various heinous misdeeds and atrocities which are not well known to the society. Moreover, the author has written this book as a means to honour and serve justice to the victims who suffered abuse and oppression under the rule of that tyrant.

All the opinions and assumptions presented in this book are the author's personal views. The author has formed most of the ideas through one of the following scenarios mentioned below:

1- The author has put himself in the shoes of Shah Jahan, the world's wealthiest emperor of that time. Nobody questions his authority as he is always right and he is doing everything under the grace of the lord.

2- The author has put himself in the shoes of ordinary people during that time. Their living conditions, and their rights, the author has tried to keep all those things in mind.

3- The author has put himself in the present times where he enjoys many rights and liberties that common citizens of that time didn't have.

Readers may find some foul language and derogatory words while reading. The author is fully aware of it and he has included them deliberately. The main reason behind it is the author's anger towards the tyrant. And also his pain and remorse for the kind-hearted people who had to suffer at the hands of that tyranny. Those derogatory terms are a means of showing his pain, outrage, and disrespect for the ruthless autocrat. The author's intention wasn't to cause any harm or disrespect towards anybody except the tyrant himself. The author simply wants to put forward the truth and reality. The author would like to apologise if any reader feels attacked while reading the book.

THANK YOU

Acknowledgements

The Author would like to express his deepest gratitude to Shubham Agarwal, Aishwarya Wanjari, Sankhashubro Nath, and the whole team of The Write Order Publications. This project could have never been completed and delivered at your doorstep without the continuous support and guidance being provided to the author by the team of professionals at The Write Order Publications.

Moreover, the author is deeply indebted to the works of authentic historians', Henry Miers Elliot (Author of the book SHAH JAHAN), Jadunath Sarkar (Author of History of Aurangzeb Vol. 1 and Vol. 2), V.A. Smith (Author of The History of India books), K.S. Lal (The Mughal Harem), B.P. Saksena (History of Shahjahan of Dilhi) and Fergus Nicoll (Shah Jahan: The Rise and Fall of the Mughal Emperor) who has done a lot of research and hard work for their books. Without their well-researched and original books, I would never be able to prove my points and finish my book. Also, I would like to thank all the individuals, authors, and journalists of various historical articles, blogs, news sites, and websites that deal with the details of the Mughal Empire, Shah Jahan, and other social topics which have been discussed in the book.

Furthermore, I would also like to acknowledge Google, Wikipedia, Internet Archive, YouTube, and several research sites available on the Internet which made it easier for me to find legitimate sources and information that helped in shaping this book; especially, the organisations which have uploaded the old books to the Internet Archive, thus helping in the preservation of those books that play a crucial role in understanding the history of India. (The books of Jadunath Sarkar, V.A. Smith, and H.M. Elliot were published over 100 years ago, making them hard to find. As of writing this book, many reference books were out of stock, even though they are listed on e-commercial sites like Amazon. But still, you will be able to find these books on the Internet Archive for free as they were published over 100 years ago. All these books fall under the public domain in many countries). The authors and every site, book, article, and research page has been mentioned in the Bibliography Page.

Thank you.

Table Of Contents

Chapter 1
Introduction 1

Chapter 2
Love or Lust 9

Chapter 3
Harem 18

Chapter 4
Court Chronicles 29

Chapter 5
Other Crimes and Atrocities of Shah Jahan 42

Chapter 6
War Crimes, Crimes Against Humanity, and Genocide 66

Chapter 7
Six Fundamental Rights 75

Chapter 8
Political Integration Of India 79

Chapter 9
The Workers of the Taj 82

Chapter 10
The Butterfly Effect 85

Chapter 11
Conclusion 107

Chapter 12

Action 118

Bibliography 134

CHAPTER 1

INTRODUCTION

Let's begin with understanding the difference between a temple and a shrine. Both of these words have the same meaning with some minor differences and are synonymous at times. A shrine is a sacred or holy place associated with or containing memorabilia of a particular revered person or thing.[1] On the other hand, a temple is also a sacred or holy place, but it is a building devoted to the worship or regarded as the dwelling place of a god or gods, or other objects of religious reverence.[2] A temple is a place dedicated to religion, while a shrine is a place dedicated to an important or holy person in society.[3] That's the basic or main difference between these two words.

A monument, on the other hand, is a statue, building, or other structure erected to commemorate a famous or notable person or event.[4] It may also be a statue or structure placed by or over a grave in memory of the dead.[4] Historical Monuments are those that are considered to be an important part of a famous individual's life, community, nation, or world's history. In this context, World Heritage Sites are natural or man-made sites, areas, or structures recognised as being of outstanding international importance and therefore these sites are given special protection. Sites are nominated to and designated by the World Heritage Convention (an organisation of UNESCO).[5]

Now, let's move on to the main part of the discussion or debate which is to be followed. The Historical Monument which is going to be discussed below is the most famous tourist site in India and one of the most popular tourist sites in the world.

Most or maybe all historical monuments, statues, historical sites, or places are built while keeping one common thing or objective in mind. And that is to remember the past and keep it alive. Most of these sites work as a mirror to society. These stupendous monuments connect us to the past, these monumental edifices tell us about the good and horrendous things that had happened in the past. Some Monuments represent peace, love, justice, equality, liberty, and many more beautiful things which are key to building a better, kind, and prosperous world. Splendid monuments like the Statue of Liberty of New York City represent freedom and democracy while the Statue of Unity of India represents unity.[6,7] On the other hand, there are monuments and places that were built to remind future generations of various injustices, massacres, and wars that had taken millions of lives of innocents, that had destroyed the peace and beauty of the world, that had rotten mankind with the disease of moral degradation which has caused so much hateful and unjustified acts for centuries.

These stunning monuments were created as a reminder, as some sort of a playback button or a magical mirror to look into the past. That magical mirror will help humankind to know the difference between good and evil. It will help us end hate with love, injustice with justice, oppression with liberty, and war with peace that will eventually lead to the creation of a better and loving world. These monuments teach us not to repeat the horrific monstrosities that were the product of hatred and injustice, ultimately resulting in world-altering wars. Hiroshima and Nagasaki Peace Memorials were built in memory of around 200,000 innocents who lost their lives in the nuclear attacks during the end of World War 2.[8] These memorials also express the hope for world peace and the ultimate elimination of all nuclear weapons.[9]

Most of these extraordinary monuments were laid on the foundations of truth, reality, or actual events and things that had happened in the past. But some of these monuments and historical buildings were built on a lie, a lie that is converted into a myth, and with time that myth has become the truth. These monuments were built by barbaric despots or powerful people who were full of hate, intolerance, ruthlessness, and mercilessness against the innocents and the weak. These uncultured swines have made countless lives endure suffering and pain, massacring millions of kind-hearted souls during their lifetime.

On top of that, these uncivilised pieces of junk had built monuments and statues of their own so that they will be remembered and their worthless glorious achievements stay alive until the end of mankind or because they must have thought that they have done the lord's work or they are the lord. These people have tried to keep their history alive by erasing and altering the true history of countless hardworking kind souls during their regime, for future generations to remember, love and worship them.

Yes, unfortunately, most of them succeeded in putting their name in modern history books and people are remembering them. However, they are not known to society for doing the lord's work but they are remembered for the atrocities and heinous crimes that they committed. Nobody worships or loves them, everybody despises them for their mercilessness, iniquities, and crimes against humanity that they did during their lifetime. Sadly, few of these wretched tyrants were able to get love and reverence from future generations long after they were gone. They were able to achieve their ultimate objective of being worshipped by future generations, at the expense of the lives and freedom of the hardworking, warm-hearted naive individuals.

The real heroes of the world, the diligent and generous people of the working class, who were the sole reason for the existence and survival of humankind, who helped in creating a better and prosperous world, and the ones who built these miraculous monumental edifices and everything else from ground up with their dedication, hard labour, and kindness have been forgotten. These compassionate people have become nameless and their history has been erased and altered by tyrannical and wicked individuals for their favours, greed, and needs. These ugly swines were able to hide their crimes, enormities, and injustices by altering and erasing the history of countless kind, hardworking souls. The Shrines of Lies of these contemptible wretches are being treated as symbols of love, peace, and harmony.

TAJ MAHAL is one of those shrines of lies and it has glorified the tyrant who built this monument. It is not treated like any other monument but it is worshipped as a symbol of true love. It is not only a monument but it has been declared one of the "New 7 Wonders of the World". The New 7 Wonders of the World were chosen in 2007 through an online contest which was organised by the Swiss Foundation known by the same name i.e. The New 7 Wonders Foundation. More than tens of millions of people voted, and approximately 100 million people voted from all over the world to choose these New 7 Wonders of the World.[10] Taj Mahal was chosen along with The Great Wall of China, Petra in Jordan, Colosseum in Rome, Chichen Itza of Mexico, Machu Picchu of Peru, and Christ the Redeemer of Brazil.[11] Along with that, UNESCO (United Nations Educational, Scientific and Cultural Organisation) also declared the Taj Mahal a World Heritage Site in 1983.[12] The man I shall be talking about is the 5th Mughal Emperor of India who is known to everybody by the name Shah Jahan. He was born on 5th January 1592 in Lahore and he died on 22nd January 1666 at Agra.[13] His reign as the Emperor of India lasted for 30 years, 5 months, and 17 days i.e. from 1628 -1658.[14] According to the official UNESCO webpage dedicated to the Taj Mahal, it is described as an immense mausoleum of white marble, built in Agra between 1631 and 1648 by order of the Mughal Emperor Shah Jahan in memory of his favourite wife Mumtaz Mahal.[15] The Taj Mahal is considered to be the greatest architectural achievement in the whole range of Indo-Islamic architecture.[15] The uniqueness of the Taj Mahal lies in some truly remarkable innovations carried out by the horticulture planners and architects of Shah Jahan.[15]

For sure, the Taj Mahal is full of beauty and stunning architecture but within that beauty lies an ugly truth. The beauty of the Taj Mahal has glorified a man who doesn't need to be glorified, it has made him worthy of respect but that man doesn't deserve to be venerated. His tomb has been worshipped like he was some saint back in his time but in reality, he wasn't a saint, he was a satan. I am 99% sure that millions of people who have voted the Taj Mahal to be one of the New 7 Seven Wonders of the World don't have any idea about who Shah Jahan actually was and what he did to the people of his empire, to the hardworking innocent citizens of India. What did he do to Mumtaz Mahal or other women?

Probably half of the people who voted for the Taj Mahal in the contest weren't even from India, these voters were probably from western countries or other parts of the world other than the Indian subcontinent. Most of these people could have just heard about the overhyped love story of Shah Jahan and Mumtaz Mahal; the architectural and scenic beauty of the Taj Mahal. But I am pretty sure, none of these individuals had any idea about the brutal reality hidden behind the spectacular opulence of the Taj Mahal. 13% of the total votes came from India, and even the Union Culture Minister of India (in 2007) at that time also casted her vote for the Taj Mahal.[16] I can assure you that the Culture Minister or the majority of these voters from India also doesn't have any idea about the dark past of Shah Jahan. If any of these people could have known the truth about the heinous crimes that he committed during his lifetime as an emperor, then none of them would have ever voted for the white edifice built by him.

Even I, who was born and raised in India, once upon a time, viewed the Taj Mahal as a symbol of true love and Shah Jahan as a true lover, a benevolent king, and a caring husband who truly loved his wife. If you read any article or visit any internet blog/site which is dedicated to the Taj Mahal, those pages just focus on the love story of Shah Jahan and Mumtaz Mahal or describe the eye-catching architectural and scenic beauty of the Taj Mahal. None of them tell us anything related to Shah Jahan's life and the things he did in his lifetime. On the official UNESCO website nothing related to the personal life of Shah Jahan is included. Even on the official government website for the Taj Mahal, nothing can be found related to the reign, government (administration), and policies of Shah Jahan (the only point mentioned there states that during Shah Jahan's rule, there was an increment in revenue demands from the peasantry, without proper explanation. There is also no mention of how it affected the peasantry in general).[17]

Same can be said about the school books of India issued by the Indian Educational Boards. As a kid, I remember that we used to have entire chapters and essays devoted to the Taj Mahal. But none of those chapters and essays dealt with the personal life of Shah Jahan and the living conditions of civilians during his reign. None of those educational books stated the truth about the crimes and injustices perpetrated by Shah Jahan on the people of India. They were just focused on glorifying this tyrant, his 'undying' love for Mumtaz Mahal and the structural beauty of the marble edifice. Stating repeatedly on how the Taj Mahal has received several awards and achievements, we started to feel proud that such a monument belongs to us Indians. However, my illusion shattered as I slowly began to unravel the dark and horrifying truth behind the white marble mausoleum complex.

As I became an adult then slowly I started to get various details of Shah Jahan's personal life and many egregious iniquities that he did during his lifetime. As a kid, I started to have several doubts and I began to ask questions (to myself) regarding Shah Jahan after learning about the cruelty of the mughal emperors, especially Aurangzeb, who was also the son of Shah Jahan. I found many people like me asking similar questions as I had through the internet and various social media platforms like Quora, Reddit, etc. As answers started pouring in, I began to question the whole legacy of Shah Jahan and the Taj Mahal. From there, my quest for the truth began and I wanted to know more and write about it.

After reading the official historical documents of his reign from the books like Shah Jahan by Henry Miers Elliot and well-researched books like Reign of Aurangzeb by Jadunath Sarkar, History of India by V.A. Smith, HISTORY OF SHAHJAHAN

OF DILHI by B.P. Saksena, Shah Jahan - The Rise and Fall of the Mughal Emperor by Fergus Nicoll, I got to know what kind of a person Shah Jahan truly was. After getting to know the truth, the guilt crept in. I felt guilty that I wanted to visit the Taj Mahal, and I felt guilty that I cared about a cruel autocrat who made countless innocent Indian citizens suffer and committed many atrocities on them. I felt guilty that I had memorised an entire essay written on Taj Mahal. All of it was a lie and always has been.

I don't know why we were not taught the truth regarding Shah Jahan and the Taj Mahal back in our school days. I have nothing against the chapters or the other things that were taught to us regarding the Taj Mahal and its fabulous architecture but against the fact that these were the only things that were taught to us at school. Why were we not taught anything regarding the personal life of Shah Jahan and the lives of people during his reign? Why the only important thing about Shah Jahan is that he truly loved Mumtaz Mahal and he built the Taj Mahal in her memory? Why has Shah Jahan been so much glorified and idolised in India? His idealisation in India has made him an international icon, his Taj Mahal has become a symbol of love while he has been idolised as a true lover, a caring husband, and a merciful king. I have been searching in vain to find the answers to these questions. But one thing is for sure which is that everything has been a beautiful illusion conjured at the whim of politics and propaganda. The beauty of the Taj Mahal has blinded everybody and the ugly truth remains hidden within the walls of the Taj Mahal. The ugly and heinous malfeasances of Shah Jahan and his reign have been buried beneath the white marble floor of the Taj Mahal.

But now all of those lies will be out. Did Shah Jahan really loved Mumtaz Mahal? What were the crimes committed by Shah Jahan? Was the Taj Mahal built out of love or out of guilt, or out of ego and arrogance? And many more questions of these sort might have arisen in your mind by now. This book may finally be able to answer those questions.

Initially supposed to be an article, this book is the product of extensive research. As I started digging into more details and research, the article just kept on getting bigger and bigger and finally, I decided to convert it into a full-length book. This book focuses on various war crimes and injustices that happened under the jurisdiction of Shah Jahan including the misdeeds which were carried out by Shah Jahan himself. Majority of the population is not familiar with the real history of Shah Jahan. They adore Shah Jahan as a true lover and worship the Taj Mahal as a monument of love. I hope that this book will be an eye-opener for them. I believe that after seeing the true face of Shah Jahan and learning the truth, these people shall be able to change their perspectives and feelings regarding Shah Jahan and the Taj Mahal just like I changed mine. If you are one of the worshippers of the Taj Mahal and Shah Jahan then this book is for you. It just might be able to make you reconsider your views regarding the Taj Mahal and Shah Jahan.

Chapter 2

Love or Lust

Did Shah Jahan ever truly love Mumtaz Mahal?

No, Shah Jahan never loved Mumtaz Mahal. It was not love, it was only lust; that's all. From our childhood, we have been told that the Taj Mahal is a symbol of love because Shah Jahan built it in the memory of his favourite wife, Mumtaz Mahal and her tomb was buried within the Taj Mahal.

First of all, Shah Jahan had 10 wives, including Mumtaz Mahal.[1] Mumtaz Mahal was one of those many wives of Shah Jahan. So if he loved her, if she was his true love, if she was the last person on earth that he would ever love and care about then why did he have to marry 9 more women? Some people have justified this act by mentioning that the other marriages that Shah Jahan had were just out of political consideration, as per the official court chroniclers of Shah Jahan. I have read the English Translated versions of two most famous court chronicles of Shah Jahan which are Badshah-nama by Abdul-L-Hamid Lahori and Shah Jahan-nama by Inayat khan and I can't find any mention of Shah Jahan's marriages and political considerations. B.P. Saksena also states that no political motive can be seen behind Prince Khurram's (Shah Jahan) marriage to the daughter of Mirza Muzaffar Husain Safavi (Saksena, 1932).[3]

However, according to another court chronicler Qazwini (Qazinivi), Shah Jahan's relationship with his other wives *"Had nothing more than the status of marriage. The intimacy, deep affection, attention and favour which His Majesty had for the Cradle of Excellence [Mumtaz] exceeded by a thousand times what he felt for any other"*.[4] The thing that most people don't understand is that these documents can't be 100% accurate. Because the annalists and authors of these documents were appointed by the King or his administration. They couldn't write freely as they were under the emperor's jurisdiction and they could only write whatever pleased the king and his administration. More details on the court chronicles will be available in the upcoming chapters.

Furthermore, Shah Jahan wasn't only in a relationship with his 10 wives but, he also had a harem built where all his wives along with female servants and concubines reside. He had this harem palace just like his ancestors, with the sole purpose of fulfilling his sexual desires and engaging in various lustful activities. According to several sources, his harem palace consisted of around 200 to several thousand women (2000 - 8000). More details about the life of women in the harem will be in the next chapter. So, if Shah Jahan truly loved Mumtaz Mahal and she was his favourite wife, then why did he have concubines and sex slaves in his harem?

Also, it is to be noted that Mumtaz Mahal died while giving birth to her 14th child with Shah Jahan. Mumtaz Mahal was born in April of 1593 as Arjumand Banu Begum in Agra to a family of Persian nobility.[5] She was engaged to Shah Jahan in 1607.[6] She got married to Shah Jahan at the age of 19 in 1612.[7] Mumtaz Mahal died on 17th June 1631 in Burhanpur Deccan.[7] She had been accompanying Shah Jahan whilst he was fighting a campaign in the Deccan.[8] She was married to Shah Jahan for 19 years. In those 19 years, she got pregnant 14 times. It means that she was basically getting pregnant every year without any considerable rest both physically and mentally. Moreover, Fergus Nicoll has said that there there isn't any historical record that states the number of intervening miscarriages that could have happened other than these 14 pregnancies (Nicoll, 2009).[9] Also, he has said that Mumtaz Mahal, while approaching the age of 40, could have been well advised by her caretakers to avoid childbirth as she had already fulfilled the primary job of providing a heir to carry on the Mughal Dynasty (Nicoll, 2009).[10] Shah Jahan could have been aware of it but he ignored it and he kept on getting her pregnant. Despite her pregnancies, she used to accompany Shah Jahan on all his campaigns and travels.

Let's look at some scientific definitions, studies, and facts related to pregnancy and maternal death first.

Maternal death is when a pregnant or birthing person dies during pregnancy or up to 42 days after the end of pregnancy from health problems related to pregnancy. Maternal death and maternal mortality mean the same thing.[11]

Neonatal death is when a baby dies in the first 28 days of life.[12]

Stillbirth is when a baby dies in the womb after 20 weeks of pregnancy. Most stillbirths happen before a pregnant person goes into labor, but a small number happen during labor and birth.[13]

Gravidity is defined as the number of times that a woman has been pregnant.[14]

The chances of having an issue with pregnancy or problems during childbirth are a little higher in a first pregnancy but there are lesser chances in a second pregnancy.[15] Moreover, the risk grows once again after five or more pregnancies.[15] A study at the University of Texas Southwestern Medical Centre has shown that just after the third delivery, a woman's arteries thicken and there is an increase in blood pumping by more than 50%, which doubles the risk of getting a heart attack.[16]

Along with that, a study at Columbia University found that there is a greater chance of Hemorrhage if a woman has given birth more than 5 times.[17] *This is a condition where, due to multiple births, the woman's womb has become inelastic and its muscles weak and they are unable to contract after the placenta is cut, leading to excessive bleeding.*[18] *In simple words, Postpartum hemorrhage (also called PPH) is when a woman has heavy bleeding after giving birth.*[19] This condition was the reason behind Mumtaz Mahal's death during her 14th pregnancy.

Furthermore, the Centre for Disease Control and Prevention and also March of Dimes recommend that a woman has to wait for 18 months after having a baby before becoming pregnant again.[20,21] It means that the baby has to be around 1 and half years of age before his/her mother gets pregnant again. If the woman becomes pregnant again before finishing her 18 months period, then there is a higher chance of premature birth.[21] From these studies, it can be said that the safe limit for a woman to keep her health and her life safe is to have no more than 3-5 kids.

The table below contains data about the Mumtaz Mahal's age during each birth, the names of her children, their date of birth, and date of death. This table is taken from the article Monument of Love or Symbol of Maternal Death: The Story Behind the Taj Mahal by Anant Kumar of Xavier Institute of Social Services, Ranchi.[22] (Note- I was unable to find the exact source of this table as per mentioned in the Reference Note of the Article. Moreover, I have also referred to Fergus Nicoll's book for double checking and to make some corrections regarding some dates and names of the children.)[23]

Year	Mumtaz's Age	Name of Children (Date of Birth- Date of Death)	Life of Children (in years)
1613	20	Hur al-Nissa Begum (30th March 1613–14 June 1616)	03
1614	21	Jahanara Begum (1st April 1614–6 September 1681)	67
1615	22	Dara Shukoh (29th March 1615–30 August 1659)	44
1616	23	Sultan Shah Shuja (2nd July 1616–1660)	44

1617	24	Roshanara (2nd September 1617–1671)	54
1618	25	Aurangzeb (3rd November 1618–21 February 1707)	89
1619	26	Ummid Baksh (16th December 1619–March 1622)	03
1621	28	Princess Thurayya (11th June 1621–28 April 1628)	07
1622	29	Shahzada (name unknown) (1622–1622)	00
1624	31	Murad Baksh (8th October 1624–14th December 1661)	37
1626	33	Luft Allah (4 November 1626–14 May 1628)	02
1628	35	Daulat Afza (9 May 1628–13 May 1629)	01
1630	37	Husn-Ara Begum (23 April 1630–died young)	00
1631	38	Gauhar-Ara Begum (17 June 1631–1706)	75

As stated earlier, Mumtaz Mahal died while giving birth to her 14th child due to the condition known as Haemorrhage. She was in unusually prolonged labour for about 30 hours.[24] Labour is more of a medical term, in simple words, we can say that she was in immense pain and suffering for 30 long hours.

From the above-mentioned table, I have made the following points. Mumtaz Mahal birthed 14 children and out of those 14 children, 1 was a stillbirth, 6 of them died in infancy while the remaining 7 survived adulthood. Among the kids who died in infancy, two of them succumbed to smallpox disease (Hur al-Nisa and Princess Thurayya).[2] Getting pregnant every year without getting proper rest from the previous pregnancies was taking a toll on Mumtaz's health. It was not only affecting the health of Mumtaz but also her babies. Shah Jahan must have seen it, he must have noticed that the health of his beloved wife was declining after every pregnancy. But still he ignored it all. It seemed like he didn't care about his wife's well being and his true love didn't matter enough to him to consider being taken care of. The 9th pregnancy of his wife resulted in a stillbirth. By this time, Shah Jahan had already lost 2 of his kids in infancy. But still, he didn't stop, he continued to have sex with her, he kept f**king her, he kept getting her pregnant. By the 13th pregnancy, Mumtaz Mahal and Shah Jahan had lost 5 of their kids in infancy and 1 was a stillbirth. The 13th one was a neonatal death, Shah Jahan did not even stop here. He ignored the fact that the poor health and multiple pregnancies of his wife were one of the reasons why half of his kids were dead now. Fergus Nicoll makes a similar point and he also states that Mumtaz Mahal never had any option given to stop her annual pregnancies (Nicoll, 2009).[10] The other and the major reason was Shah Jahan himself. By the next year, he made his beloved and favourite wife pregnant again for the 14th time. Finally, after the 14th pregnancy of his wife, he stopped. Wow, the unstoppable fathering machine Shah Jahan stopped. At last, maybe he could have gotten to know what it feels like to get pregnant, bear children and go into labour every year. How it could have felt to go into prolonged labour for 30 hours. Finally, Shah Jahan, like a true lover and a caring husband, started to care about his beloved, the most favourite wife. But there was one little problem and the problem was that she was gone, she died while giving birth to the 14th child of Shah Jahan. She was in labour for 30 hours, 30 f**king hours.

To make this beautiful love story more romantic and simplistic. Let's assume that Mumtaz Mahal was one of the multitudinous sex toys and child-bearing machines in Shah Jahan's factory of lust. In his factory of lust and carnal desires which is known as the harem, Mumtaz Mahal was the most likeable childbearing and lust-appealing machine. Shah Jahan liked to operate that machine by himself all the time. That machine was made to fulfil his horniness under the veil of true love. He was the only one who had the authorization to use it as he was the one who set that authority. Shah Jahan loved to operate that machine and he kept on using it. He kept on using it without any service or maintenance. After bearing the first child, it started to give some issues but still, Shah Jahan started using it immediately. Shah Jahan didn't even care to notice the issues as the machine was still working and it was still performing the main duty which it was supposed to do. That major duty was to produce children for Shah Jahan's Dynasty even though half of the products made by that machine came out to be defective. Shah Jahan kept pushing it to its limits without maintenance, as the machine did not resist, did not speak, did not tell him to stop, did not ask him to send it for repair.

Finally, one day all those small problems and troubles converted into one major issue while the machine was in the final process of making the 14th child of Shah Jahan. The machine broke, and all of its parts and its switches came out. At that moment, Shah Jahan called the mechanics and the servicemen to service and repair the machine. But the machine had been crushed down and it was non-repairable. It was a sad day for Shah Jahan, as he lost his favourite sex toy and child-bearing machine but still, he had a 100s like more of those machines. That machine was Mumtaz Mahal.

Shah Jahan also had 2 more kids with his other 2 wives.[25] Moreover Dr. A. L. Srivastava claims that Shah Jahan had 18 children.[33] On top of that, there is a chance that Shah Jahan also had kids with his concubines in his harem and this dark part of his life has been totally whitewashed from the pages of history. This is the reason why I was not able to find any information regarding the concubines and slave girls of the harem during Shah Jahan's reign. Fergus Nicoll in his book Shah Jahan - The Rise and Fall of the Mughal Emperor quotes regarding the Shah Jahan and any accident children which could have been born as a result of his sexual relationship with his concubines as *"Any accidental children, by-blows of dalliances with harem concubines, were to be ignored, reduced to the status of anonymous minor aristocracy and kept in their place with deliberately parsimonious allowances"* (Nicoll, 2009, p. 171).[26] The famous Indian historiographer K. S. Lal in his book The Mughal Harem has said the following regarding Mumtaz Mahal *"Shia by conviction, Persian through parentage, this Mughal queen lived like a Hindu princess, devoted to her husband and family and suffering all the while, producing one child almost year"*(Lal, 1988, p. 83).[27] Furthermore, K. S. Lal has also said that even though Shah Jahan built the Taj Mahal to show his dedication and undying love for Mumtaz Mahal but the various scandals rule out any exclusive devotion to her (basically he was indicating towards his sensual pursuits, seraglio, incest, and other immoral acts).[28]

It is also to be noted that even in ancient times and in mediaeval India, people used to practise various birth control methods.[29,30] Also, there is mention of the abortion being carried out in the mughal harem.[31] Looking at the number of times Mumtaz Mahal has been getting pregnant, Shah Jahan could have asked Mumtaz Mahal to practise these birth control methods. It seems like he didn't do it or even if Mumtaz Mahal wanted to practise these methods, he didn't give her permission. He just ignored it. Yes, for sure those birth control methods were not that effective and safe but at least Shah Jahan could have given those methods a try if he really cared about the well-being of his wife.[32] He could have asked his hakims and European physicians to do some research on the birth control methods in a bid to develop some new, effective and safe birth control methods. He could have also asked them to find a cure for smallpox which was the main cause behind the death of his two kids. He could have done it without facing any type of difficulty like lack of resources or funds as he was the wealthiest emperor in the world during his reign. Also when he was just a Prince, he still had access to the imperial resources and wealth rewarded to him by his father which he could have used and invested (just a portion of it) in medical research but he didn't. He could have done it if he really loved her, if she really mattered to him. Frankly, if she really mattered to him, he couldn't have made her pregnant 14 times or kept f**king her and making her pregnant until she died giving birth to his children. Directly, it can be said that Shah Jahan was responsible for Mumtaz's death. His negligence towards the mental and physical health condition of his wife eventually led to her maternal death. Indirectly, it can be said that his hunger for sex and lust killed Mumtaz Mahal. Shah Jahan murdered the supposed true love of his life due to his venereal desires. He was also indirectly responsible for the death of the 7 children that he had with Mumtaz Mahal.

CHAPTER 3
HAREM

In the old times, a harem was the separate part of a Muslim household reserved for wives, concubines, and female servants.[1] The harem which will be discussed in the upcoming paragraphs is solely related to Mughal Emperors and it revolves mostly around the harem of Shah Jahan. This Mughal Harem is basically the private residence or palace of the emperor where all the women related to the emperor lived. Every mughal emperor had a harem. The Shah Jahan's seraglio is also known as Khas Mahal and it is located in Agra.[2] He also had a harem in Old Delhi which became the capital city of his empire after Agra. Multiple sources indicate that his harem consisted of around 200 to several thousand women (probably around 2000 - 8000).[2,3,8] I am not able to find the exact number or an original source that could be able to give the exact number of females who inhabited Shah Jahan's harem. But many European Travellers (i.e. Thomas Roe, Thomas Coryat, Robert Coverte) have stated that Shah Jahan's father Jahangir had around 1000 concubines in his harem while in the book The Mughal Harem by K.S Lal, it is mentioned that Jahangir had around 300 females in his harem.[4,5] Shah Jahan's grandfather Akbar had around 5000 women in his harem.[6] Another European traveller and physician Niccolao Manucci (1638 -1717) has claimed that Shah Jahan had 2000 women in his harem.[7,8] Harems of Shah Jahan's ancestors like Babur and Humayun had around 200 women in their harems while after the accession of Akbar followed by his successors Jahangir and Shah Jahan, the harems got bigger in size and a lot of women started to reside in them.[9] It wouldn't be a surprise if Shah Jahan also used to have that number of women in his seraglio if we compare it with his father and grandfather. The number collectively includes all of his wives, maids, his mistresses, and also women slaves.

Moreover, Manucci, Bernier, and Mundy had also noticed that Shah Jahan just like his ancestors also used to organise a festival called Khusroz or Navroz, or fancy(mina) bazaar festival which was attended by crowds of women.[10] Manucci has said that the main reason behind this festival was to look for the most beautiful women for Shah Jahan and if Shah Jahan found any women attractive in the crowd, matrons (female officers) and eunuchs of the harem used to present that woman to the royal palace in front of the emperor.[10,11] A eunuch is a man who has been castrated, especially (in the past) one employed to guard the women's living areas at an oriental court.[12] These matrons and eunuchs also worked as spies for the emperor and the princes to give information about the most beautiful females that were found in the empire and also to lure those women into the harem by any means so as to make them the emperor's concubines and servants.[13,14] It is also stated by European Travellers.[13,14]

On top of that when Shah Jahan attacked the Portuguese colony at Hugli in 1632, many beautiful captured European women were sent into the Shah Jahan's harem while the other women which were not that attractive or the emperor didn't find them to be desirable enough were distributed among the umara (noblemen) and princes.[15] This incident has also been mentioned in the official court chronicles of Shah Jahan.[16] Nobles and officers of the Empire also had their own zenana palaces where they used to abuse girls and women.[17] In 1563, Akbar tried to end this abduction by issuing an order that prohibits the capture and enslavement of women during war campaigns.[17] Moreover, Jahangir also issued a similar decree which prohibits collectors and other officials of the empire to marry women in their districts without the king's permission.[17] If we look at the above-mentioned incident of women enslavement, it doesn't look like Shah Jahan followed the steps of his grandfather to end this abduction, instead, he did it by himself and under his jurisdiction. Also, I did not find any mention of any order or farman (in any of the books or articles on the internet related to his reign which I read) issued by Shah

Jahan that prohibits this practice of women abduction and enslavement. From here, it can be said that Shah Jahan used to abduct women, and also the women were enslaved and abused during his reign. This point (opinion) will be easily proven in the upcoming chapters.

All of these women residing in the harem had different jobs but there was one job that was the most important among all. That job was to take care of the emperor and look after him. Taking care of the emperor does not only mean that it only includes taking care of his physical health, his diet, doing his laundry, cleaning his room, and preparing his favourite meals. The one job that was above all these above-mentioned jobs, the job that was the top priority and that was the most important job as per the emperor's wishes. That job was to fulfil the erotic desires and fantasies of the emperor by any means, anything intimate or any sexual favours that can be given to the emperor. They have to do anything that the potentate wants them to do. If he wanted them to have sexual intercourse with him then they have to, if he wanted them to dance or sing naked then they had to, if he wanted them to bath him naked then they had to, if he wanted them to entertain him then they had to, if his commanders or officials wanted to have any kind of sexual relation with any of these ladies of the seraglio and the emperor had given them permission to do so, then those women were presented to them as their sexual slaves to perform various salacious activities as desired by the officials.[18] It was never the women's choice, it was always Shah Jahan's choices, his wishes, and desires.

The two main concubines of Shah Jahan were Akbarabadi Mahall and Fatehpuri Mahall. Both of them stayed with him in the prison along with the rest of the harem until his death in 1666.[19] Shah Jahan also built an entire mosque which is known as Fatehpuri Mosque in Delhi to show his affection and love towards his favourite concubine Fatehpuri Mahall.[20] From here, it can be easily interpreted that Mumtaz Mahal wasn't Shah Jahan's only love, and the Taj Mahal wasn't the only monument that Shah Jahan built to show his affection and undying love for

Mumtaz. The only difference is that the Taj Mahal got worldwide attention and recognition as compared to the Fatehpuri Mosque. The alleged lust story of the Fatehpuri Mosque remained underrated while the 'love story' behind the Taj Mahal became overrated.

It is said that the women residing inside the harem used to live a luxurious lifestyle as compared to the common women and the citizens of Shah Jahan's empire.[21,22] The women used to get an annual salary and the amount of that salary entirely depended on their relationship with the emperor, their closeness to the emperor, and the emperor's likeness towards them.[23,24,25] What I can't understand is what type of luxurious life was that if the women were not allowed to leave the zenana palace even though they were being provided everything inside it or whatever the emperor wished them to have.[26] If they wished to go outside, they couldn't leave the seraglio whenever they wanted.[26] The annual salary which these ladies receive doesn't make any sense then as they can't spend this money by going outside to the nearby bazaar (market), any festival or social event.

As for the Emperor, these women were his property. Regarding the harem Fergus Nicoll has said that "*The harem may have been comfortable, even luxurious but it was a gilded cage*" (Nicoll, 2009, p. 73).[27] If some women are lucky enough to get permission to go outside the harem, they have to follow various rules and regulations which were probably set up by the emperor and his administration.[26] The most important rule among those was the seclusion of women from public observation and to do so, they had to wear purdah which would cover (hide) their entire bodies.[28] Also, the emperor can take the women who he wants to go out with him while going hunting or on any campaign. While travelling with the sovereign they still had to wear the purdah.[29] No matter what their own wishes were, no matter what religion they belonged to, no matter how hot it was outside, or if the clothing was too sensitive or irritating to their skin, they had to wear it all the time.

Another rule was that all the women residing in the harem were forbidden to indulge in any kind of bond or sexual relationship with men.[30,31] They do not have any sexual life. All the women were sexually deprived. Their sexual deprivation can be easily proven from the various incidents that were described by the European travellers, mainly physicians and doctors who had permission to enter the seraglio to check their health and treat the women who got ill in the harem.[32] Niccolao Manucci has said that sometimes the women in the seraglio used to hold his hand to softly bite or kiss it and some of them even put his hand on their breast through the curtain when he visited them for their health checkups and treatment.[32] It happened to him several times but he had pretended not to notice it or it had never happened in a bid to stop any kind of suspicion regarding sexual attraction between him and the women among the harem guards who were always present when he was running his health tests.[32] Sometimes, women also use to fake illnesses just for this purpose.[33] All the women have to stay loyal to the emperor as everything in the harem belongs to the emperor, it's his property. This was the reason why all the guards who were assigned to guard the harem were eunuchs.[34,35] Eunuchs of the harem were also used to smuggle men into the seraglio for women.[36] Moreover, Manucci has said that eunuchs were also used by the harem women for erotic pleasures.[36]

There were also women guards surrounding the harem.[37] Even if any woman who was brave enough to seek freedom by trying to run away or expressing her feelings with another woman or eunuch about her carnal desires and relationships, running away motives and leaving that hell, she puts herself in immense danger. As many eunuchs and ladies in the seraglio were also spies, they could inform the guards and the potentate about the intentions of these women in the harem who were planning to run away or are having an intimate relationship with eunuchs or any man from the outside world.[38,39,40,41] These brave women then could have had to face brutal punishments, jail times, or even death sentences or beheadings as per the wishes of the emperor.[42] Even if the emperor dies, these women were still not allowed to leave the harem lifestyle as they got obliged to the new emperor.[43,44] The harem ladies of the deceased emperor were shifted to other places.[43] The widows of the dead emperor and older ladies used to have separate compartments in the seraglio and they didn't have any visitors other than the women of the harem or the emperor himself if he liked them.[44,45] Any woman to go into the harem, had to make that harem her whole world. They would have to cut ties to their family and the outside world. The harem becomes the only world in which they exist and whether they liked it or not, they had to stay in it and eventually die in that world.

It is ironic that Shah Jahan wanted the women of his harem to cover all of their bodies i.e. wear a purdah while going outside to protect them from the dirty eyes of perverted men and save their dignity and self-respect. Yet he was the one, who was that perverted man, he was the one who was disrespecting them, he was the one who was taking away their dignity. He was making them dance naked, bathe him naked, or telling them to indulge in various other lustful activities which will fulfil his horniness. Shah Jahan wanted those women to not have any relationships as he wanted them to stay loyal to him but he was the one who was being disloyal to them, to his own wives. He was the one who committed adultery. He was the one who was sleeping or having sex with other women, his concubines, underage girls, and sex slaves. I will not be surprised even if he had sex with other women right in front of his true love of life, Mumtaz Mahal. His true love could have watched him f**king those women or underage girls like a f**king dog. It is stated that only 5% of the total number of females residing in the harem were used for sexual favours.[44,46,47] But it doesn't mean that only those 5% of women will have to spend the rest of their lives giving sensual pleasures to the emperor, that 5% of women kept on changing, that 5% of women could be anyone, that 5% of women could be from anywhere.

For example, if you are a servant in the harem or any other female in his empire and you just seem to pass by the Shah Jahan's royal carriage and he finds you more attractive and arousing than one of his concubines, then you will become his next pleasure toy, and that mistress could become a servant. That was one of the reasons behind the Navroz or Khusroz festivities being organised by the emperor just for the search of new beautiful women to replace the old ones or the ones which the emperor has used over 100% and now he doesn't view them as attractive anymore. That's the reason why matrons and eunuchs also used to keep on searching for beautiful girls in the empire so that those women would be able to replace the old concubines and the women sex slaves which the emperor does not find attractive anymore.

Also, another deduction that can be easily drawn from this is that Emperor Shah Jahan raped many or all the females in the harem, no woman wanted to have sex with him but they had no other choice. Nobody during that time questioned the Emperor Shah Jahan. No woman resisted or raised her voice against the debauched autarch as all of them feared for their lives and also the lives of their families and loved ones. The Emperor Shah Jahan was above laws and regulations as he was the one who was setting up all these laws and regulations. Nobody questioned his ethics, his morals, and his principles just like his ancestors who also had harems and who also had sex with hundreds or thousands of women, who also treated women like lust toys or childbearing machines.

On top of that Shah Jahan was the only Mughal Emperor who was accused of incest. Farzana Begum who was the sister of Mumtaz Mahal was the mistress of Shah Jahan.[48] Manucci has said that Shah Jahan was also having intimate relationships with the wives of his officials.[48,50] French physician and traveller Francois Bernier (1620 - 1688) has said that Shah Jahan was in a sexual relationship with his own daughter Jahangara because she resembled Mumtaz Mahal-his favourite lust doll.[48,49,50] On top of that, this obscene act was approved by the scoundrelous religious advocates of Shah Jahan who stated that *"it would have been unjust to deny the King the privilege of gathering fruit from the tree he had himself planted"* (Saksena, 1932, p. 338).[50] British traveller and trader Peter Mundy (1597 - 1667) has also said the same.[48,51] Many historians have denied their accusations because of a lack of evidence regarding it and also it is believed that this accusation is totally based on the bazaar gossip of that time.[52,53]

On the other hand, there were also some historiographers like Vincent Arthur Smith who believed it to be true.[52,53] According to the historian Banarsi Prasad Saksena, a lack of evidence that would be sufficient enough to prove these remarks to be true or false is impossible (Saksena, 1932, p. 337).[52,53] Maybe he could have just raped her just like hundreds or maybe even thousands of other women. There is no documentation which claims that the women in the harem willingly or liked to have sex and engage in libidinous activities with the emperor. Also, I could not discover anything related to the lives of women and their views regarding the emperor and the harem in the Shah Jahan-nama and Badshah-nama court chronicles. Even if something is mentioned regarding the seraglio in other court chronicles, then that thing will mainly focus on the lavish lifestyle and the luxuries being offered to the women in the harem. None of those records will ever tell us the truth and show the reality, as free speech during that time was just a dream, a word that doesn't even exist in dictionaries.

I know what you people might be thinking right now. How the author is accusing Shah Jahan of raping women and having sex with his own daughter? Before answering this question, let's take a look at the remarks made by various chroniclers and European travellers regarding the harem and erotic pleasures of Shah Jahan. Bernier has said that Shah Jahan was fond of fair sex and he used to keep dancing girls called Kanchens the whole night in his harem during every festival that happened during his reign.[54] Johann Mandelslo (1616 - 1644) was a German traveller who stated that Shah Jahan loved to enjoy Naked Dances.[55,56] K. S. Lal in his book The Mughal Harem has said that Shah Jahan's aberrations attracted adverse comments (mainly because of his harem, sexual desires, and licentious nature).[57] Also, Shah Jahan was the only Mughal Emperor to be ever accused of Incest.[58] K. S. Lal states that one of the reasons behind Shah Jahan's excessive sensual desires was due to the absence of senior ladies in his harem.[59] His mother died in 1619, his grandmother died in 1621, and his wife Mumtaz Mahal died in 1631.[59] Due to the absence of these senior ladies, there wasn't any other female head who had influence and power enough to question and prevent Shah Jahan's excessive debauchery and to stop him from becoming a sex addict.

The famous historian V.A. Smith regarding Shah Jahan quotes that "*There is no doubt that during the remaining thirty-five years of his life he disgraced himself by gross licentiousness*" (Smith, 1919, p. 415).[60] Manucci has said that the harem was a prison house for women.[61] Manucci and Bernier has described Shah Jahan as an individual whose only concern in life was to indulge in bestial sensuality and monstrous lewdness (Saksena, 1932).[62] Both of them has also claimed that Shah Jahan had weakness for the flesh (Bernier) and the only thing which he cared about was to keep looking for women to fulfill his sexual fantasies (Manucci).[58] K. S. Lal calls the mughal harem a "stable" for women which was established to satisfy the lust of kings and nobles (Lal, 1988, p. 204).[63] K.S. Lal concludes his book by stating that the main purpose of the harem was to provide pleasure to the king or the society's elite (Lal, 1988).[64] Dr. A. L. Srivastava mentions that Bundela lady prisoners who were introduced into the Shah Jahan's mughal harem had to pass their days in "gilded misery" (Srivastava, 1986).[65] Shah Jahan was born and raised in the mughal emperor's family. He could have learned most of the things from his ancestors and also his parents failed to teach him the basic ethics, morals, and etiquettes. After becoming the emperor, his administration failed to teach him these things or his administration never questioned his decisions, moralities, and ethics. Due to this, he could have built an image of being the lord himself. Shah Jahan could have believed that whatever he did was always right and perfect, and all the decisions, laws, and rules that he made were the best. He could have never tried to even ask the women residing in the seraglio about what they actually wanted. Even though if he did ask, he could have gotten the answer that he wanted to hear and if some brave woman had said the truth to him it could have felt like somebody spitting right to his face. Then he could have made her suffer because his arrogance made him believe that he was always right and the best. He could have never taken the permission of the women or his wives to have sex with him. He couldn't even have the words like consent or rape in his dictionary. His power, enormous wealth, influence, and authority over everybody else in the empire was able to make him take advantage of countless innocent women who were full of helplessness. On top of that, he could have added hopelessness to their helplessness. Shah Jahan was not the wealthiest emperor, but he was the world's most affluent abuser of his time.

Some people will state that during those times every king and all the rich elites used to have big harems where all their wives, concubines, servants, and girl slaves used to live. It was pretty common during those times so it doesn't make any sense for the author to question Shah Jahan's lifestyle in the harem with his wives , concubines, and sex slaves. I just wanted to say that if something wicked and heinous was common during the old times, it doesn't mean that it was right and acceptable, that we shouldn't question it, we don't need to criticise it, and there is no need to protest against it. This is totally wrong because all the liberties and rights which we are enjoying today came into effect after a lot of criticism, protests, and revolutions. If nobody had criticised monarchies and dictatorships as those were pretty common in the past then we could have never been able to taste the fruits of freedom and democracy, we could have still being treated like shit, we could have still be getting abused and slaughtered at the hands of tyrannical despots and scoundrelous swines like Shah Jahan in these present times.

The same thing applies to the mughal harem, sexual slavery, and other disgraceful things that used to happen in the past. But still, if you don't agree with me and you still think the author is just making a big deal out of it. If you think that we should put this thing under the rug, we should never focus on it; If people stop criticising and protesting against evil, atrocious, and unlawful things because those crimes are becoming common because of this kind of ideology. Then it will worsen the moral degradation of society. For e.g.- If 7 out of 10 women are getting raped and nobody protests against it as it is getting common, then in the long term the future of the entire human civilisation will be doomed. Because the trauma experienced by those poor unlucky women will not only affect their mental and physical health but the guilt and pain of not getting justice will make it worse. Also, the health of their kids or any future babies they were going to have gets vulnerable to this. If those babies or kids were having mental health issues and trauma, then the future of the human race will suffer from that trauma too as those kids will turn into adults one day. Also, many criminals had traumatic experiences as kids or have mental health issues, and the transgressions committed by them lead to the moral degeneracy of the entire society.* So please think wisely and carefully before trying to put this Shah Jahan's harem thing under the rug. That's enough for now I wanted to say regarding this point.

*Note- The author is not trying to condone or justify the acts and crimes committed by criminals. The primary and major source for most of the information and facts related to the Harem is K. S. Lal's The Mughal Harem book which was published in 1988. Kishori Saran Lal (1920- 2002) was an Indian historian.[66] This book is entirely based on the Mughal Harem and it is heavily researched. It presents the most accurate description and understanding of the Mughal Seraglio.

CHAPTER 4

COURT CHRONICLES

The term "court chronicles" refers to scholarly accounts of kingdoms, their courtiers, and common people's living conditions.[1] Most kings had court chroniclers who kept meticulous records of events during their reign.[1] Simply put, these are basically kind of autobiographies, biographies or a memoir of kings and emperors of old times. Shah Jahan also had these court chronicles written during his reign to serve as the official documents portraying the historical events and things that happened during his time of reign.

One of the most famous court chronicle of Shah Jahan is **Badshah-nama** written by Abdul Hamid Lahori which contains the 20 years of history of Shah Jahan's reign.[2] The other famous court chronicle is known as **Shah Jahan-nama** by Inayat Khan and it contains 30 years of history of Shah Jahan's reign.[3] I have read the translated versions of both of these court chronicles in English. The name of the translated book is SHAH JAHAN and this book is available in the Cornell University Library.[4] The author of the book is Sir Henry Miers Elliot (1808-1853) who was an English historian and he worked with the East India Company for 26 years.[5] The original Abdul Hamid Lahori Badshah-nama itself contains 1662 pages while Shah Jahan-nama of Inayat Khan contains 360 pages (360 leaves) of 19 lines each.[6,7] There are works of other authors too which also contain the same number of pages and are bulky as Badshah-nama and Shah Jahan-nama which have been translated in this book. But H.M. Elliot's book Shah Jahan just has 156 total pages. From here, it can be said that the translated version does not translate the whole text of the court chronicles exactly line by line. Instead, it provides an overall summary of many of those documents and it just focuses on the major historical events that happened during Shah Jahan's reign. I would say probably those events which H.M. Elliot could have thought to be important as he was the author of this book. Also, H.M. Elliot has himself said that the work (talking about Badshah-nama) contains a lot of details that don't matter to anyone other than the nobles and courtiers of that time.[8] The same thing can also be said about the other works too. There is a chance that some details and events could have been missing or were not translated and being provided in this book. But still, I was able to extract a lot of details regarding various heinous crimes and atrocities committed by Shah Jahan from this book.

Shah Jahan was not only a prurient sex predator and lustful king but he was also a barbaric tyrant. He was not a peace-loving king in fact he was the one who hated it the most. In the court chronicles, Shah Jahan has been shown as a peace-loving and merciful king, an emperor who truly cares about his people and his administration; he has been referred to as a generous and world-conquering monarch. The chroniclers of these historical records have tried so hard to build a positive and charming image of Shah Jahan, they have tried their best to glorify him and they did try to present him in the best magnificent way that was ever possible. In these documents, the authors have done a lot of flattery and boasting for the emperor so as to please him and make him happy. Regarding the portrayal and characterization of Shah Jahan by his writers of court chroniclers, B.P. Saksena states that *"They condone his faults, and justify some of his darkest deeds on the grounds of the public and political morality of the time. Thus according to their picture Shahjahan appears as a virtuous and affable sovereign with hardly a blemish in his character worth mentioning"* (Saksena, 1932, p. 336).[9]

I don't blame them for this because that was the only option available to them. These authors work under the eye of the emperor or his administration because they were basically appointed by them. They can only document those historical events which the emperor wants them to write about. They can write those things and events in such a way that will help in showing the king as a great ruler and a magnificent achiever. They have to be very careful while writing these documents as if they have written something that doesn't portray the emperor as a great ruler or it can spoil the reputation of the potentate, or if the emperor himself doesn't get pleased by it and he doesn't like it; then that event or that description has to be amended, rewritten, or erased from the record as per the emperor's wishes. If these writers or courtiers resist doing so, then they have to face dire punishments, jail times, even death sentences or beheadings. It all depends upon the nature of the emperor like what sort of an animal or a heartless tyrant he is.

As I have said earlier, the official records written during Shah Jahan's reign portray Shah Jahan as a merciful and loving emperor. But the reality is far from what had been shown and written in those court chronicles. Shah Jahan was not a kind of ruler who would serve his people but he was an emperor who wanted to rule and conquer. He was not a giver, he was a taker. He tried to take everything from the people wherever he laid his eyes on. He didn't want to build a better, peaceful, and unified empire. He didn't focus on creating better living conditions for his people. His only aim in life was to conquer all of India (consisting of the Republic of India, Pakistan and Bangladesh). That's the only thing which he focused on during his lifetime.

During his reign of 30 years (i.e. 1628 - 1658), he spent most of his time as a fierce autarch fighting and conquering the independent states and forts around his empire. His court chronicles present him as a great warrior as well as a great emperor with a third eye. An emperor who had always made the best decisions. No matter how hard these authors of Shah Jahan have tried to hide, amend or bury his atrocities and countless horrendous crimes. But still, if anybody reads these official histories of Shah Jahan, it will not be hard for them to find descriptions of many wicked deeds and gruesome outrages committed by Shah Jahan and his Imperial Army against the weak, the hardworking, and the peace-loving citizens. In the upcoming paragraphs, the translated description of the countless heinous malefactions of Shah Jahan has been taken from the book named Shah Jahan written by Sir Henry Miers

Elliot.

Note- To make it easier for you, I have also included the Page numbers from where I have gotten that text from the book. You can read that book to get a better understanding of what's really happening. Italic Text implies that I have copy-pasted the same text as it is from the book.

BADSHAH-NAMA by Abdul Hamid Lahori [12]

Shah Jahan became the next Mughal emperor on 6th February 1628 AD. He ascended the throne in the city of Agra.[10] As per the record, the first year of Shah Jahan's reign began on 6th February and the second year of Shah Jahan's reign began on 20th December in the same year i.e. 1628 AD.[11]

3rd YEAR OF THE REIGN (1629 AD)

Conquest of Nasik, Trimbak and Sangamner

"Sher Khan, Subadar of Gujarat, joined with 26,000 men, and the Khwaja sent him to attack the fort of Batora, in the vicinity of Chandor, near Nasik and Trimbak. Sher Khan ravaged the country, and returned with great spoil." (Page 11)

CAMPAIGN AGAINST NIZAM SHAH AND KHAN-JAHAN

"The Khwaja then sent detached forces into the hills, and also into the inhabited country, and they returned from each raid with abundance of corn and other necessaries, having killed or taking prisoners many of the enemy." (Page 12)

5th YEAR OF THE REIGN (1631 AD)

Fight for Bijapur

"With this intention the royal army marched along the bank of the Kishan Gang to Raibagh and Miraj, two of the richest places in that country. Wherever they found supplies they rested, and parties were sent out to plunder in all directions. On whatever road they went they killed and made prisoners, and ravaged and laid waste on both sides. From the time of their entering the territories to the time of their departure they kept up this devastation and plunder. The best

part of the country was trodden under, and so, the forces had recovered strength and the rains were near..." (Page 33)

CAPTURE OF THE PORT OF HUGLI

"*On the 2nd Zi-1 hijja, 1041, the attack was made on the Firingis by the boatmen on the river, and by the forces on land. An inhabited place outside of the ditch was taken and plundered, and the occupants were slain. Detachments were then ordered to the villages and places on both sides of the river, so that all the Christians found there might be sent to hell. Having killed or captured all the infidels...*" (Page 36)

Note- I have included this passage as an attempt to show the religious fanaticism, hate, and bigotry of Shah Jahan and his Imperial Army towards other religions.

6th YEAR OF THE REIGN (1632 AD)

DESTRUCTION OF HINDU TEMPLES

"*It had been brought to the notice of His Majesty that during the late reign many idol temples had been begun, but remained unfinished, at Benares, the great stronghold of infidelity. The infidels were now desirous of completing them. His Majesty, the defender of the faith, gave orders that at Benares, and throughout all his dominions in every place, all temples that had been begun should be cast down. It was now reported from the province of Allahabad that seventy-six temples had been destroyed in the district of Benares.*" (Page 39)

CONQUEST OF DAULATABAD

"*Fath Khan now woke up from his sleep of heedlessness and security. He saw that Daulatabad could not resist the Imperial arms and the vigour of the Imperial commander. To save the honour of his own and Nizam Shah's women, he sent his eldest son Abdu-r Rusul to Khan-khanan...*" (Page 44)

"*CHRISTIAN PRISONERS (Text, vol.i.p.534) on the 11th Muharram, (1043 A.H.), Kasim Khan and Bahadur Kambu brought... 400 Christian prisoners*, male and female, young and old, with the idols of their worship, to the presence of the faith-defending Emperor. He ordered that the principles of the Muhammadan religion* should be explained to them and that they should be called upon to adopt it. A few appreciated the honour offered to them and embraced the faith they experienced the kindness of the Emperor. But the majority in perversity and wilfulness rejected the proposal. These were distributed among the amirs, who were directed to keep these despicable wretches in rigorous confinement. When any one of them accepted the true faith, a report was to be made to the Emperor, so that provision might be made for him. Those who refused were to be kept in continual confinement. So it came to pass that many of them passed from prison to hell. Such of their idols as were likenesses of the prophets were thrown into the Jumna, the rest were broken to pieces." (Page 45)

*Note- The correct number of prisoners should be 4400 not 400.[20]

8th YEAR OF THE REIGN (1634 AD)

Rebellion of Jajhar Singh Bundela and his son Bikramajit

"The hot pursuit allowed the rebels no time to perform the rite of Jauhar, which is one of the benighted practices of Hindustan. In their despair they inflicted two wounds with a dagger on Rani Parbati, the chief wife of Raja Nar Singh Deo, and having stabbed the other women and children with swords and daggers, they were about to make off when the pursuers came up and put many of them to the sword. Khan-dauran then arrived, and slew many who were endeavouring to escape. Durgbahan, son of Jajhar, and Durjan Sal, son of Bikramajit, were made prisoners. Udbahan, and his brother Siyam Dawa, sons of Jajhar, who had fled towards Golkonda were soon afterwards taken. Under the direction of Khan-dauran, Rani Parbati and the other wounded women were raised from the ground and carried to Firoz Jang. The royal army then encamped on the edge of a tank... While they rested there, information was brought that Jajhar and Bikramajit, ... were killed with great cruelty by the Gonds who inhabit that country... Khan-dauran rode forth to seek their bodies, and having found them, cut off their heads and sent them to Court.... When they arrived, the Emperor ordered them to be hung up over the gate of Sehur." (Page 54)

9th YEAR OF THE REIGN (1635 AD)

"On the 15th Sha'ban Khan-dauran came from Chanda to wait upon the Emperor. He presented... the wives of the wretched Jajhar, Durgbahan his son, and Durjan Sal, his grandson. By the Emperor's order they were made Musalmans by the names of Islam Kuli, and 'Ali Kuli. and they were both placed in the charge of Firoz Khan Nazir. Rani Parbati, being severely wounded, was passed over; the other women were sent to attend upon the ladies of the Imperial palace." (Page 55)

DESPATCH OF THE IMPERIAL ARMY AGAINST SAHU AND OTHER NIZAM-SHAHIS

"Udbihan, the son of Jajhar, and his younger brother, Siyam Dawa, who had fled to Golkonda, were made prisoners by Kutbu-1 Mulk, and were sent In custody to the Emperor. They arrived on the 7th Shawwal. The young boy was ordered to be made a Musalman, and to be placed in charge of Firoz Khan Nazir, along with the son of Bikramajit. Udbihan and Siyam Dawa, who were of full age, were offered the alternative of Islam or death. They chose the latter, and were sent to hell." (Page 57)

Note- The young boy mentioned over here is associated with Nizamu-l Mulk's family who was given the same name as that of Nizamu-l Mulk. Nizamu-l Mulk was the king of Ahmadnagar. (Page 56)

SHAHJAHAN-NAMA by Inayat Khan[13]

22nd YEAR OF THE REIGN (1648 AD)

Loss of Kandahar

"During the period of the siege, which extended over two months, nearly 2,000 of the Kazalbash army and 400 of the garrison were slain." (Page 100)

Note- I have included this text so as to give an estimate of the number of lives lost during the meaningless war campaigns of Shah Jahan which were only done to fulfill his haughtiness, arrogance, and undying greed asking for more and more.

28th YEAR OF THE REIGN (1653 AD- 1654 AD)

"Appointment of 'Allami to the task of demolishing the Fort of Chitor, and Chastising the Rana"

"On his arriving within twelve kos of Chitor, which is the frontier of the Rana's territory, inasmuch as the latter's negotiations had not yet been satisfactorily terminated, he commenced plundering and devasting, and depasturing his cattle on the crops. On the 5th of Zi-1 hijja, this year, having reached the environs of Chitor, he directed working parties with pickaxes and spades to overthrow that powerful stronghold. Accordingly, in the course of fourteen or fifteen days, they laid its towers and battlements in ruins, having dug up and subverted both the old and the new walls, levelled the whole to the ground. The Rana having awoke from his sleep of heedlessness at the advent of the prosperous banners at Ajmir, the irresistible force of the royal aims, the dispersion of the peasantry, and the ruin of his territory, sent off a letter containing the humblest apologies to Court..." (Page 111)

29th YEAR OF THE REIGN (1654 AD-1655 AD)

CAMPAIGN IN SIRMOR

"Among the incidents of the past year, the appointment and despatch of Khalilu-lla Khan during the return from Ajmir, with 8000 men, for the purpose of coercing the Zamindar of Srinagar, and capturing the Dun, have been already detailed by the historic pen..." (Page 112)

"On reaching Bahadur Khanpur, which is a place belonging to the Dun and lies between the rivers Jumna and Ganges, in consequence of the peasantry that dwelt in that neighbourhood having taken refuge in the hills and forests and defiles, and obstinately refusing to return, he despatched the ever-triumphant troops from every side to coerce them, who succeeded in inflicting suitable chastisement. A number of the rebels therefore fell by the sword of vengeance, and many more were taken, prisoners; after which the remainder tendered their allegiance, and innumerable herds of cattle fell into the hands of the soldiery..." (Page 113)

30th YEAR OF THE REIGN (1655 AD-1656 AD)

"*Appointment of prince muhammad aurangzeb to conduct the campaign of bijapur, and dismissal, of mu'azzam khan (mir jumla), etc. From the presence*"

"*As Mu'azzam Khan had reported that he had sent several led horses, adorned with diamonds... to Adil Khan, the Shah Buland Ikbal despatched by the hands of two confidential slaves a mandate, agreeably to orders...*" (Page 128)

AMAL-I SALIH by Muhammad Salih Kambu[14]

This work is sometimes called SHAH JAHAN-NAMA.[15]

31st YEAR OF THE REIGN

"*Mu'azzam Khan Joins Aurangzeb. Capture of several fortresses belonging to Bijapur. Defeat of 'Adil Khan's army.*"

Fight for the Fort of Bidar

"*The brave assailants took advantage of this accident, and pouring into the fortress on all sides, they killed or bore down all who resisted, and raised the flag of victory...*" (Page 133)

"*Intelligence reached the Prince (Aurangzeb) that large bodies of the forces of 'Adil Khan were collecting at Kulbarga, and preparing for war. He consequently sent Mahabat Khan with fifteen thousand well-mounted veteran cavalry to chastise these forces, and not to leave one trace of cultivation in that country. Every building and habitation was to be thrown down, and the land was to be made a dwelling for the owls and kites.*" (Page 134)

"*Mahabat Khan then ravaged Kalyani, and continued his march.*" (Page 135)

OTHER INCIDENTS RELATED TO PILLAGING, KILLING, and CAPTUREMENT OF POWs as mentioned in the court chronicles.[16]

(Page 16)- A number of Afghan men and women were made prisoners by the Imperial Army.

(Page 18)- At the fort of Tilangi, The Royal Army captured around 500 prisoners of war.

(Page 18) - Bakir Khan, ravaged the country around Kherapara.

(Page 22)- Shah Jahan's army commander was ordered to plunder the town (fort) of Dharur in Dakhin.

(Page 24) - Raja Jai Singh was sent to despoil and ravage the town and Petta during the attack on Parenda Fortress.

(Page 26) - Shah Jahan's army General Azam Khan, pillaged the town and fort of Balni.

BIJAPUR CAMPAIGNS[17]

(Page 31, Page 60) - The imperial army ransacked Sultanpur and Kulbarga country.

(Page 46) - Pillaging done at Daulatabad.

(Page 56) - Shah Jahan ordered his army generals to attack and ravage the country (Bijapur) of Adil Khan. (I believe the territories which were attacked and destroyed were Nander, Kandahar, Forts of Udgir, and Usa)

(Page 57)- Shah Jahan gave orders to ravage the Bijapur territories by sending his army generals in three different directions.

(Page 58, Page 61)- A similar Imperial Order was again given which allowed the Imperial Army to kill and devastate as much as it can in the Bijapur territory. Each and every inhabited place which came in the way of Shah Jahan's Army General Khan Zaman was vandalised.

(Page 69) - The Imperial Army started to plunder when they entered a fort during the Conquest of Tibet.

(Page 76) - Another incident which shows the moral degradation of the Imperial Army was that in Balkh, the soldiers started looting and oppressing the people of this region.

(Page 121, Page 122) - The Imperial army captured the many soldiers (POWs) of Kutbu-l Mulk during the Golkonda campaign.

(Page 136) - When the Aurangzeb marched against Kalyani, he attacked and captured the fort of Kalyani. All the garrison of the fort was allowed to march out with their wives, families, and property. The main reason given in the court chronicles behind this action was that the whole garrison were followers of the same religion that was the state religion of Shah Jahan's Empire. From here, another point regarding Shah Jahan's religious intolerance and bigotry towards other religions can be proved because the only reason the garrison of the fort was allowed to march out without getting pillaged, enslaved, or killed was religion. If the garrison belonged to a different religion, then they could not have been spared their lives and their property and women could have been taken by the Imperial Army as trophies.

SYNOPSIS

From these above-mentioned paragraphs and lines taken from the translated version of the official court chronicles of Shah Jahan, it can be said that the Shah Jahan committed various heinous crimes and atrocities on the populace of India. Along with that, under his jurisdiction, his army chiefs and the imperial army did various disgraceful and horrific acts on the enemy soldiers as well as on the common innocent civilians. I don't even have to explain anything in those court chronicles as everything is written in simple language but still, I have written a small elaborated summary of the text which I have read and taken from the court chronicles in the next paragraph.

Shah Jahan court chronicles literally states that the Imperial Army used to kill people and ravage lands, property, and whatever thing that comes up in its way. Shah Jahan, his commanders and the Imperial Army also used to plunder and steal as much as they could from the ordinary people during several war campaigns. Maybe, that's the reason why Shah Jahan became the wealthiest emperor of that time. Shah Jahan was never the wealthiest emperor, he always had been the wealthiest thief of his time. Moreover, the army under the jurisdiction of Shah Jahan also used to take hostages and prisoners of war. The captured women were made to attend the harem where they were probably being used as things existing only for the purpose of pleasure, entertainment, and also as sex slaves for the lecherous Shah Jahan and his commanders.

Along with that, there was also mention of the forceful conversion of religion. The prisoners of war if belonging to a different group of religion were asked to change their religion and follow the religion which Shah Jahan follows. If those people didn't accept this proposal, then they were to face hard and brutal punishments and torture until they die out of immense pain or they accept the state religion. The captured children of the enemies and prisoners were made to convert their religion to the state religion without their permission. Along with that, there is also mention of the presence of slaves in the Imperial Army and in the Mughal Empire. Furthermore, religious places and statues belonging to other religions or which represented a different religion other than the state religion followed by Shah Jahan were vandalised and desecrated by the orders of Shah Jahan.

Just looking at the information that had been provided in those translated versions of official court chronicles of Shah Jahan, even though a lot of details could still be missing from those court chronicles as they just show an overall summary of the original text. Also, these court chronicles could be just the tip of the iceberg as there could have been much worse atrocities and hideous things that happened during Shah Jahan's reign which were never documented. These court chronicles just focus on the emperor and his glorious achievements which in fact were horrific and flagitious crimes in the name of those marvelous accomplishments. But in the eyes of the Shah Jahan, those were his outstanding achievements as he did the lord's work under the grace of the lord. Moreover, nothing related to the life of ordinary citizens can be found in those court chronicles as it seems like the life and the living conditions of those common people did not mattered enough to be considered worthy of being documented in those court chronicles. Even though there is little mention of deadly famine in these court chronicles but it has just been mentioned for the sole purpose of exaltation and idealisation of Shah Jahan.[18] The description of famine in these court chronicles totally contradicts with the eye witness accounts of famine provided by European traveller Peter Mundy.[19] Shah Jahan can easily be charged with committing various war crimes, crimes against humanity, and genocides. He can be easily declared as a war criminal because he has literally documented these severe wrongdoings in his court chronicles. From here, it wouldn't be hard for anybody to accept that Shah Jahan was the wealthiest oppressor in the world during his reign.

I have also noted another thing from the Badshah-nama and Shah Jahan-nama court chronicles, which is that Shah Jahan's so-called 'true love' or his 'favourite wife' Mumtaz Mahal has just been mentioned once in the entire text of these documents. To be precise, it wasn't even her who has been mentioned. It was her death that had been mentioned and also that she bore 14 kids to Shah Jahan. Wow, the 'true love' of Shah Jahan has just been mentioned once in his most famous historical books. Basically, Shah Jahan was a secret lover or a kind of ghost lover of his 'favourite wife' who didn't want to tell or reveal how much he loved her, how much he cared about her; to the future generations who were gonna read these court chronicles. But for sure he put all of his love and caring nature towards his wife in the Taj Mahal just after her death. In my opinion, she didn't mattered enough for Shah Jahan to be considered getting importance and mention in his court chronicles, preferably the most famous and important ones.

Chapter 5

Other Crimes and Atrocities of Shah Jahan

The above-mentioned vicious crimes and atrocities committed by Shah Jahan have only been taken from the official records of his reign. There could be hundreds or thousands more of these misdeeds and injustices that had happened during his reign. But all of those egregious crimes and wrongdoings have been erased from history. Shah Jahan doesn't want future generations to know about those atrocities. Some of those horrific crimes are mentioned below which are taken from various authentic historical books and articles dealing with the reign of Shah Jahan and the Mughal Empire.

I have read the books History of Aurangzeb, Vol 1- Reign of Shah Jahan, and Vol 2- War of Succession by Jadunath Sarkar, History of India by V.A. Smith, Shah Jahan- The Rise and Fall of the Mughal Emperor by Fergus Nicoll, HISTORY OF SHAHJAHAN OF DILHI by Banarsi Prasad Saksena and The Shah Jahan Handbook by Ricardo Mcgee.

Note- The text has been paraphrased and you could also find some more words in the paraphrased text in some points. It has been done to give the readers a better understanding of the text. Also, the paraphrased text may have been a little influenced by all the books and articles which the author had read. It doesn't mean that the author had developed his own fictional text and quotes to prove his points, all the paraphrased text is 100% verifiable. I have also included the page numbers of the books from where I have gotten the information to make it easier for you to compare the facts and have a better understanding if you ever want to read these books.

Book- HISTORY OF AURANGZEB, VOLUME 1- REIGN OF SHAH JAHAN

By Jadunath Sarkar

Mainly based on Persian Sources

Jadunath Sarkar (1870 - 1958) was an Indian historian and specialist on the Mughal Dynasty.[1]

This book is based on original sources and documents of that time. The official language of the Mughal Regime was Persian which makes the content and details mentioned in these books to be true and authentic as these books heavily relies on the Persian documents of that time.[2] These two books primarily deal with the various war campaigns as the main focus of these books is Aurangzeb. But still from these books preferably the Volume 1, I was able to discover some more crimes and atrocious incidents that happened during the reign of Shah Jahan, some of those were listed below as follows:

ATTACK ON BUNDELA- In 1635, Shah Jahan's Imperial Army attacked Bundela and the Imperial Army was able to wound and capture the ladies and other personnel of the Bundela family. It has also been mentioned in his court chronicles. Jadunath Sarkar quotes about the incident as

"A more terrible fate awaited the captive ladies who survived: mothers and daughters of kings, they were robbed of their religion, and forced to lead the infamous life of the Mughal harem,* – to be the unloved plaything of their master's passion for a day or two and then to be doomed to sigh out their days like bond women, without knowing the dignity of a wife or the joy of a mother. Sweeter far for them would have been death from the hands of their dear ones than submission to a race that knew no generosity to the fallen, no chivalry to the weaker sex." (Sarkar, 1919, p. 27).[3]

Along with that, when Shah Jahan visited the Bundela capital after conquering the country, he ordered the demolition of a massive temple next to the king's palace and built a mosque over there. (Page 29)[4]

Note- Dr. A.L. Srivastava in his book The Mughul Empire also mentions that other temples and shrines in Bundelkhand were wantonly desecrated and demolished by the Shah Jahan's army.[19]

BIJAPUR FIGHT- It happened during 1636, during the fight for Bijapur, Khan-i-Dauran, one of the army commanders of Shah Jahan killed 2000 inhabitants at the Kalyan village. On top of that his other general Khan-i-Zaman sold 2000 prisoners of war which included men and women into slavery in the Kolhapur district. (Page 37)[5]

Note-This incident has also been mentioned in the official court chronicles Badshah-nama of Abdul Hamid Lahori, though it is not that much detailed.[6]

The Mughal Subahdar also captured the wife of the Maratha General Kheloji Bundela of the Bijapur Sultan. The Mughal Subahdar asked for a ransom of 4 lakh rupees from the Maratha General by telling him that if he wanted to save his honour and also the honour and chastity of his wife then he had to give that amount of money. From here it can be said that Shah Jahan's commanders use unjustified, horrific, nasty, and disgraceful methods such as capturing women of the enemy and using them as blackmailing instruments to fulfil their demands and force the enemy to surrender. (Page 55)[7]

In October 1634, Shah Jahan forbade the practice of intermarriages between hindus and muslims in Kashmir. He ordered every hindu man who has married a muslim woman to embrace his state religion or let her go so that she could be able to marry a man who belongs to her religion. This order was strictly enforced. (Page 62 and 63)[8]

Moreover, his son Aurangzeb demolished a religious place belonging to a different religion other than the state religion in the village of Sattarah near Aurangabad. (Page 171)[9]

DECAY AND MISERY OF MUGHAL DECCAN

Jadunath Sarkar also mentioned that the condition of the working class has not been improved as they had not been taken care of properly in the Deccan. Due to this many cultivators have left the mughal deccan and much of the cultivated land has been turned into jungles. (Jadunath Sarkar own words *"But agriculture had not been promoted, the peasantry had not been cherished, and new lands had not been brought under tillage. On the contrary, much cultivated soil had lapsed into the jungle, the cultivators had declined in number and resources, and the revenue had fallen off greatly."* (Sarkar, 1912, pp. 176-177))[10]

Note- In Fergus Nicoll's book, it is stated that these cultivators and peasants has joined the sovereign states which are in rebellion against the Mughal Empire.[11]

Shah Jahan's general Kahn-i-Dauran tortured and abused the collectors and peasantry in order to increase the revenue from the Mughal Deccan. The main reason behind it was to send money to the Empire instead of asking for it and to make Shah Jahan happy. (Page 180)[12]

(V.A. Smith also talks about the ill treatment of the Deccan Inhabitants by Khan-i-Dauran and overall poor condition of the peasantry in his book "The History of India")[13]

Jadunath Sarkar calls Shah Jahan a bigot due to his numerous religious intolerant policies. (Page 249)[14]

After ravaging the Bijapur territory, Mahabat Khan and the Imperial Army took all the possessions, arms, and slave girls as captives that they found in the Bijapur camp. (Page 269 and 274)[15]

After that, the Imperial Army ravaged the country up to Kulbarga. (Page 276)[16]

Note-These accounts have also been mentioned in the official court chronicles of Shah Jahan.[17]

Aurangzeb ordered the destruction of villages and slaughter of the inhabitants of Shivaji territories without any mercy or pity. Along with that he also told his officers to loot as much as they can and as they wished from them without showing any mercy. (Page 283)[18]

Book- HISTORY OF AURANGZEB, VOLUME 2- WAR OF SUCCESSION

By Jadunath Sarkar

Mainly based on Persian Sources

Jadunath Sarkar mentions that Shah Jahan had a force of 1500 soldiers who were foreign slaves. (Page 78)[1]

Shah Jahan also had slave female soldiers known as the Tartar slave women for his defence as well as for the security of his harem. (Page 84)[2]

Book- THE OXFORD HISTORY OF INDIA

By Vincent Arthur Smith

Part 6 - The Mogul Empire (Page 321-468)

Vincent Arthur Smith(1848-1920) was an Irish indologist and historian who published various books and articles related to the history of India.[1] I have read the book The Oxford History of India by Vincent Arthur Smith. This book is also well researched just like the Jadunath Sarkar ones. The best part which I loved about this work is that I was able to obtain some details regarding the miserable and poor living conditions of the working class, peasantry etc. during the reign of Shah Jahan. I was craving for that information as I was not able to find that info anywhere in the court chronicles, Jadunath Sarkar books or on the whole internet (The information regarding the living conditions of the working class in the Jadunath Sarkar books and on the internet is not enough and it is also not much detailed as compared to the V.A. Smith books). I have gathered the following information regarding Shah Jahan from this historical book.

Thomas Roe (1581-1644) was the English Diplomat of England.[2] He arrived in India during the reign of Jahangir and he made the following description of Shah Jahan who was just a young prince at that time. Thomas Roe said that Shah Jahan was filled with excessive pride and contempt for all. He doesn't show or have any respect for others. (Page 383)[3]

Along with that, Thomas Roe also calls Shah Jahan a hater of all Christians, proud, subtle, false, and barbarously tyrannous. (Page 384)[4]

V.A. Smith describes the famous peacock throne of Shah Jahan which cost around 10 million rupees during that time as follows: "*The work was a senseless exhibition of barbaric ostentation, and almost devoid of artistic merit*" (Smith, 1919, p. 393)[5]

This statement can easily be proven with all incidents of plundering and marauding mentioned in the official court chronicles of Shah Jahan.[6]

Famine in Gujarat and Deccan (1630-1632) - As I have said earlier that the Famine has been mentioned in the official histories of Shah Jahan for the sole purpose of glorification and gratification of Shah Jahan and his reign. The court chronicles state that during the famine, the kind emperor Shah Jahan distributed 1 Lakh rupees over the course of 20 weeks, distributing 5000 rupees each Monday.[7] Moreover, Shah Jahan ordered his officials to distribute another 50000 rupees in the city of Ahmadabad and he also ordered to open soup kitchens to help the people.[7] Along with that, the 'wise' and 'generous' emperor ordered to remit the 1/11th of the total tax in the famine- struck region (Elliot, 1875).[7] One point to be noted here is that the total revenue of Shah Jahan's Empire which consisted of 14 Provinces was around 19 crore rupees (1 crore equals 10 million) (Nicoll, 2009, p. 198).[8] Gujarat and Deccan were both separate provinces. From here, it can be easily concluded that Shah Jahan didn't even donate like 1% of the total revenue to these poor and hardworking inhabitants of these provinces who were brutally hit by the deadly famine. It was a formality, more of a publicity stunt, a way to fill his court chronicles, to glorify and dignify himself, and an attempt to cover his injustices and remorseless savageries than to actually provide support and help to these poor souls who were the sole reason behind that revenue.

As the whole revenue was generated and taken from the working class but still they weren't able to get mild treatment from the emperor during the Famine. Ironically, Shah Jahan wasted around 10 million rupees just to build a throne made of precious stones to delight his ego and flaunt his inequitable opulence. In Badshah-nama, it is written that the peacock throne was made only to render one service which was to adorn the throne of Empire and also to make the Majesty shine with increased brilliancy (Elliot, 1875, pp. 48-49).[9]

Clearly, the 'kind' Shah Jahan had his priorities straight where he was willing to expend a bulk of the revenue of his Empire with the main objective of serving the 'greater good', not out of his 'ego' and 'arrogance'. Those priorities and important things did not include the working class and hard working citizens of his Empire. The peacock throne for sure had helped the poor, labourers and working class to gain 'confidence' and 'trust' in their emperor who was able to afford luxurious, wealthy and healthy lifestyle, who was able to spend millions of rupees on precious stones and gems to fulfil his hobbies, pleasures, ego and arrogance.

If these people hadn't paid taxes even during the famine; their emperor, the so-called people's king or I would say the *Father of Abuse* would not be able to accumulate that much wealth and luxuries. Their hard work, their diligence, their sacrifices, their miserable living conditions, the injustices which they have to suffer, inequalities that they had to endure, the religious extremism which oppressed them, the plundering of their houses and towns; All was just a way of showing obedience, respect, and trust to their emperor, to their master, to the owner of their lives, to the looter of their hard work, rights, justice and their freedom. Because that was their life, that was their destiny, that's the reason why they were created, that was their responsibility to take care of their overlord, their owner, because that was the lord's wish as per the Emperor Shah Jahan.

Other Crimes and Atrocites of Shah Jahan

(Revenue Calculation- Many Internet Sources states that the revenue of the Shah Jahan's Empire was around 21 or 21.15 crore rupees.[10,11] Jadunath Sarkar states the total revenue to be around 20 crore rupees in 1648 (Sarkar, 1919, p. 16).[12] Sources in Fergus Nicoll's book mentions that revenue was 18.7 crore rupees (Muhammad Sharif Hanafi's, point 3, Page 299), Nawaz Khan (point 5, Page 299) puts the number at 22.5 crore rupees.[13] As per my calculations from H.M. Elliot's Shah Jahan (Muhammad Sharif Hanafi, Page 147), the revenue of the Shah Jahan's empire comes around 15.6 crore rupees.[14] The official Taj Mahal's website puts the revenue at 20 million sterling (I have calculated that amount to be around 15.7 crores).[15] I have taken the average of these numbers and rounded it off, which gives us the revenue amount number to be 19 crore rupees (Fergus Nicoll also uses this amount)[16] which I have considered and mentioned in the text above).

Peter Mundy, an English traveller and merchant who was present in India during the time of famine portrays a different eyewitness picture than what has been presented in the official records of Shah Jahan's reign. According to Mundy, the way between Surat and Burhanpur was filled with corpses and it was hard for him to find a small space for his tent. The dead bodies of all sexes and ages were being dragged naked in many towns in a bid to clear the path. It was so bad that the people prevented travelling out of fear of being eaten. But on the other side of the story, the camp of the so-called merciful and caring Emperor Shah Jahan at Burhanpur was filled with all supplies and luxuries of all types. Peter Mundy does not see anything or any kind of work done by Shah Jahan or his government to help these ill-fated citizens. On top of that, the Emperor still tried to extract tenth-eleventh of the land revenue from the famine-suffering inhabitants. The only thing the government did was that it remitted one-eleventh of the land revenue. V.A. Smith also states that there is no information about how far Shah Jahan and his administration went to get the tenth eleventh of the land revenue from the poor, weak, and famine-stricken inhabitants of the Deccan and Gujarat. Also there isn't any data available about the aftermath of famine. (Page 393-394)[17]

V.A. Smith calls Shah Jahan the *Pitiless Grandson of Akbar* due to various heinous and atrocious acts that Shah Jahan and his generals perpetrated during the Bijapur Campaign. (Page 399)[18]

CHITTOR- Shah Jahan was able to make Rana Jagat Singh of Chittor surrender with the help of brutal and cruel destruction of his territory. (Page 403)[19]

Note- This incident has also been mentioned in H.M. Elliot's SHAH JAHAN Book[20]

V.A. Smith says that the working class was cruelly oppressed in the Deccan due to the poor management of Shah Jahan's government. (Page 404)[21]

Another case of Shah Jahan's religious discrimination or religious fanaticism can be seen from the act of the Raja of Chandragiri, the representative of Vijayanagar who offered to become a follower of the state religion of Shah Jahan. He made this offer in a bid to gain the protection for his kingdom from the Mughal Emperor. (Page 407)[22]

LICENTIOUSNESS- As Shah Jahan was a lubricious emperor addicted to several lustful activities and sexual desires. So after the death of Mumtaz Mahal, his favourite sex doll, he became crazy in terms of having sex. As the historian V.A. Smith quotes regarding his lascivious manners

"*There is no doubt that during the remaining thirty five years of his life he disgraced himself by gross Licentiousness*" (Smith, 1919, p. 415)[23]

Regarding the justice done by Shah Jahan, V.A. Smith quotes that "*it appears that Shahjahan's 'justice' was merely the savage, unfeeling ferocity of the ordinary Asiatic despot, exercised without respect of persons, and without the slightest tincture of compassion*" (Smith, 1919, p. 416).[24]

Other Crimes and Atrocites of Shah Jahan

From here, it can be said that Shah Jahan's cruel and brutal justice was just meant for the rebels, petty thieves, or lower rank corrupt officials. His brutal justice fades away or it never went on to grab the necks of the powerful and high-ranking officials like Khan-i-Dauran, the governor of Mughal Deccan.[25]

Shah Jahan loved to watch the suffering and abuse of victims getting killed, slaughtered, and dying in front of his eyes. (Page 416)[24]

This was the reason why Shah Jahan has also been called a MURDERER. (I am not sure if Edward Terry called him that or it was Thomas Roe who said it, the paragraph regarding it in the book is kinda confusing) (Page 416)[24]

Following in the footsteps of their cruel sovereign monarch, the governors and local administrators also followed the same policy of indiscriminate exterminations and atrocities which were done without any proper trial to tackle and control crime instead of finding the causes of crime to end it in a long term. Peter Mundy records that in a couple of months there was a massacre of about 8000 people who were thought to be criminals, thieves, or rebels and their heads were being mounted to pillars in the Cawnpore (Kanpur) District. (Page 416- 417)[26]

CONDITION OF THE WORKING CLASS

Francois Bernier sheds light on the poor condition of the working class and peasantry during the reign of Shah Jahan. He talks about the northern parts of the country. He says that the maltreatment of the working class done by the local governors and administration is extremely worse. The local administration was so morally decayed as it deprived the working class, peasantry, and labourers of basic necessities of life and left them to die and starve out of misery and suffering. It is so worse that the inhabitants of these regions have to leave their homes and go to some other regions where they could be able to get a milder treatment. He further says that the whole country was badly cultivated due to the corrupted and tyrannous administration of Shah Jahan. Due to this, nobody was willing to or seems to care about the canals and ditches that need repairs which will eventually help in irrigation and make use of unproductive land. The houses of the people were also not in a good condition. Those houses were falling apart and tearing down and there were only a few people who were able to repair those houses or build new ones.

The country and the condition of the working class has worsened due to the very high amount of taxes which these people had to pay so that the rich, the tyrannous, the emperor, and the royal members of the empire could be able to live and afford a luxurious life and maintain his splendorous court, pay his greedy governors and administration, and also pay the large army which is used in keeping these people in subjection. The revolts and uprising against this tyranny and miserable treatment has just been prevented due to the presence of the military in these regions. Moreover, he also adds that the working class had to keep working under tyranny and poor conditions only because the cudgel and whip compel them to do so. They don't have any other option. (Page 418)[27]

A persian writer has also described the corrupt and tyrannous officials and revenue collectors of Shah Jahan as men who extract oil out of sand. Their greed and undying appetite asking for more and more from the working class was never gonna end or stop with the presence of their crowd of harpies of women, children, and slaves. (Page 418)[28]

In 1632, Shah Jahan forbade the erection of new temples during his reign. It was the reason why there were no important Hindu buildings, religious or secular sites which were found or built during his reign as per V.A. Smith. (Page 421)[29]

(It is also stated that repair of the old temples was also prohibited. This order was issued in 1633 (Saksena, 1932))[30]

V.A. Smith concludes his book by saying that the stable and organised empire built by Akbar with the help of religious toleration policy was weakened by the erroneous and religious intolerant policies of Shah Jahan and later his son Aurangzzeb. It eventually led to the collapse of the Empire after their reigns were over. (Page 466)[31]

V.A. Smith has said that Shah Jahan was cruel, treacherous, and unscrupulous in terms of running his Empire. (Page 415)[32]

V.A. Smith also describes Shah Jahan as a stern, ruthless man. (Page 465)[33]

Book- THE OXFORD STUDENT'S HISTORY OF INDIA (9th Edition)

By Vincent Arthur Smith

Revised by H.G. Rawlinson

Part 4- The Mughal Empire from A.D. 1526 - 1761 (Page 151- 235)

I have read another book too and basically it's the same as the previous book. The only difference is, it has a lesser number of pages, less detailed and is a revised edition. I was able to extract some more information from this book.

CAPTURED PORTUGUESE AT AGRA (Probably around 1632)- Around 4000 - 5000 Portuguese prisoners were brought to Agra and over there they were treated with great cruelty. Bernier describes their misery, cruel, and inhumane treatment as *"unparalleled in the history of modern times"*. (The Portguese committed some evil deeds like piracy and slave trade due to which they were attacked at Hugli.) From here, Shah Jahan's cruel, pitiless, and religious extremist nature can be observed. (Page 199)[1]

Jean-Baptiste Tavernier (1605-1689) was a French traveller who was mainly an admirer of Shah Jahan and his reign. Even he states that *"Shah Jahan by degrees murdered all those who from having shown affection for his nephew had made themselves suspects, and the early years of his reign were marked by cruelties which have much tarnished his memory."* (Page 200)[2]

Shah Jahan has been described as treacherous, cruel, sensual, and avaricious. (Page 200)[2]

Shah Jahan's enormous wealth and spectacular monuments were built on the ill-treatment of hardworking citizens who were abused by 100s of official oppressors of the empire. (Page 203)[3]

A Hindu chronicler has described the Mughal Empire as "*a system of organised brigandage*". (Page 203)[3]

Shah Jahan in confinement was "*allowed plenty of dancing-girls, and lived a voluptuous life until January 1666, when he died at the age of seventy -four*" (Smith, 1921, p. 204).[4]

V.A. Smith in the conclusion states that "*Shah Jahan revived the old evil policy of persecution, harrying the Christians and razing temples to the ground*"(Smith, 1921, p. 221).[5]

Note- Akbar abolished and illegalised the practice of capture and enslavement of Prisoners of War in 1563. (Page 184)[6]

Book- SHAH JAHAN: THE RISE AND FALL OF THE MUGHAL EMPEROR

By Fergus Nicoll

This book is another well-researched and original work regarding the reign and life of Shah Jahan. This book doesn't focus entirely on Shah Jahan but it also focuses on Jahangir and Aurangzeb. Overall, the author's views on Shah Jahan are neutral but still, in some scenarios, the author has criticised Shah Jahan. I was able to extract some more incidents portraying the heinous crimes of Shah Jahan from this book.

In the preface of the book, the author has stated that Shah Jahan reigned like an *enlightened despot* and the author has called Shah Jahan a *monster of moral depravity*. (Page ix)[1]

The author describes Shah Jahan as a clever, ruthless, arrogant young prince. (Page 74)[2]

Other Crimes and Atrocites of Shah Jahan

In 1614 during the Mewar campaign, Prince Shah Jahan's generals in Udaipur sabotaged the worshipping places belonging to other religions. (Page 89)[3]

In 1622, Prince Shah Jahan rebelled against Jahangir for the Mughal Throne and he attacked Agra with his army. Shah Jahan and his army committed various atrocities on the inhabitants of Agra out of frustration because he was not able to enter the Agra Fort. Italian traveller Pietro Della Valle who was at Surat during the attack has said, *"that his army and himself (Shah Jahan) had committed very great cruelties there in spoiling and discovering the goods and money of the citizens; particularly that he had tortured and indecently mangled women of quality and done other like barbarities, whereby he rendered himself very odious to the people."* (Page 127)[4]

Fergus Nicoll states that *"Needless to say, the empire was divided between a very few 'haves' and a great many 'have-nots'."* (Nicoll, 2009, p. 199).[5]

The Dutch trader, Francisco Pelsaert describes the condition of the working class in Shah Jahan's reign as that the peasants faced a bleak existence, cruelly and pitilessly oppressed. Such oppression is exceedingly prevalent in this country. (Page 199)[6]

Chandrabhan the Brahmin counsellor has claimed that the Mughal State was careful to look after its most valued citizens. (Page 200)[7]

On Pages 198-200, the author basically tries to portray the presence of unjustified wealth inequality in Shah Jahan's reign. For example- In 1636, a labourer in Surat or a domestic servant in Agra was getting an annual salary of 25 rupees with a maximum of 50 rupees. On the other hand, the princes, begums, nobles, officers, and other members of the aristocracy received 18 million rupees out of the total revenue of 190 million rupees (1628-1629) while the rest of the annual proceeds used to go into imperial coffers as crown land revenue.[8]

Fergus Nicoll in the conclusion of his book writes *"Yet, as father to his great nation, Shah Jahan had shown no greater concern for the sufferings of the poor than other rulers of his time"* (Nicoll, 2009, p. 247).[9]

Book- THE SHAH JAHAN HANDBOOK: EVERYTHING YOU NEED TO KNOW ABOUT SHAH JAHAN

By Ricardo Mcgee

Another book about the reign of Shah Jahan is THE SHAH JAHAN HANDBOOK written by Ricardo Mcgee. This book depicts numerous facts and incidents related to Shah Jahan and his reign. The details or the facts are not in sequence as the handbook keeps on jumping forwards and backwards in the reign's time period but still, I was able to extract some more information regarding other wicked deeds of Shah Jahan which I was not able to find from the V.A. Smith, Jadunath Sarkar and Fergus Nicoll's books.

Note- This book was hard to acquire but still I was able to get a hold of the E-Book version of it on Kobo. Many facts in the E-Book version are repeated multiple times. I am not sure if that's how the book actually is or if the E-Book version is not properly created.

MEWAR BATTLE - In 1615 during the reign of Jahangir, the Imperial Army under the command of Prince Shah Jahan was sent to win and besiege the independent kingdom of Mewar. When Shah Jahan went over there, he brutally ravaged the territory of Mewar, lives of innocents were taken, property of Mewar was burnt down and devastated. Many religious places belonging to other religions were destroyed. Women and children were captured and brutally tortured in a bid to compel the ruler of Mewar Maharana Amar Singh to surrender to the Mughal Empire. Finally, the Raja (King) surrendered to the emperor and a deal was made in 1615 with Shah Jahan. (Page 36 of 52, Introduction)[1]

(In Fergus Nicoll's book, it is also stated that captured inhabitants of the Mewar were being sold into slavery. (Page 87))[2]

SLAVERY- Under the reign of Shah Jahan, peasants, labourers, and other members of the working class were forced to sell their women and children if they were not able to pay the required taxes to the emperor. Moreover, Shah Jahan also ordered that these women and children had to be sold especially to the rich members, lords, and officials of his state religion. Along with that the revenue collectors or officials were allowed to enslave these poor oppressed peasants. As per the book, this is also mentioned in one of the official court chronicles of Shah Jahan i.e. Qazinivi. The Augustinian missionary Fray Sebastiao Manrique who was in Bengal in 1629-1630 and again in 1640 also mentions this point. (Page 6 of 60, Shah Jahan 3)[3]

Note- The same point has been mentioned though less detailed in Fergus Nicoll's book on Page 199.[4]

DESTRUCTION OF GURDWARA- In 1632, Shah Jahan ordered the vandalisation of a Gurdwara and Baoli (a sacred well) at Lahore. Thousands of lives were lost during the battles between Sikhs and the Imperial Army at Amritsar, Kartarpur, and other places in the regions of Punjab. (Page 25 of 60)[5]

SATI AND OTHER EVIL CUSTOMS - Mughal Emperors did not interfere too much with evil customs but they tried to end Sati. According to Jean Baptiste Tavernier, in the reign of Shah Jahan, widowed women with children were not allowed to perform sati but still, the corrupted generals and officials of Shah Jahan's reign used to give permission to perform this hideous practice after taking bribes. (Page 30 of 60)[6]

Book- HISTORY OF SHAHJAHAN OF DILHI

By Banarsi Prasad Saksena

Banarsi Prasad Saksena was a historian associated with Allahabad University.[1] His book is also well-researched and genuinely reliable. Mostly the book deals with various war campaigns and rebellions during the reign of Shah Jahan. Along with that, the book also sheds light on the history of some independent states. Overall, the author's opinion towards

Shah Jahan and his reign are favourable but still at some parts in the book, the author has criticised Shah Jahan. From this book, I found some more horrific brutalities and religious bigotry steps taken by Shah Jahan during his reign. Moreover, I have read this book at the end of my research, so most of the atrocious incidents in this book have already been mentioned by me from other books that I had read early.

Johann Mandelslo (1616-1644) was a German Traveller who stated that during the occasion of Tazias, devotees of other religions were forbidden to appear in the streets of Agra. (Page x x iii)[2]

At Khirki during the Deccan Campaign, the Imperial army desecrated and destroyed every building which was erected over there in the last 15 years. (Page 29)[3]

Prince Shah Jahan plundered Amer during his rebellion against his father Jahangir. (Page 46)[4]

In 1629, during the rebellion of Jujhar Singh, Shah Jahan's generals ruined the country of Orchha. (Page 81-82)[5]

B.P. Saksena calls Shah Jahan a ROBBER. This comment was made after Shah Jahan asked for money from Jujhar (Jajhar) Singh to forgive him for his offences. Also, this statement could have been influenced by several acts of plundering which were carried out by Shah Jahan and his Imperial Army during various war campaigns. (B.P. Saksena's words *"But money could secure forgiveness for everything ; it could sanctify even his darkest deeds. The Emperor says not a word about recompense to the heirs of Prem Narayan. He wants only money for himself. In other words, he wished like a robber to share the spoils of a brother robber, and not like a King to defend his own subject. The fact is that he coveted Jujhar Singh's illgotten gains, and wanted a pretext to deprive him of them."* (Saksena, 1932, p. 85)[6]

Shah Jahan ordered the demolition of a religious place belonging to a different religion in Orchha. (Page 89-90)[7]

Other Crimes and Atrocites of Shah Jahan

Shah Jahan ordered the execution of a Zamindar and without any shame or pity he ordered that his wife should be given to one of the officers of his state religion. (Page 117)[8]

In 1641, During the Palamau Campaign in Bihar, The Imperial Army ruthlessly and without any mercy destroyed the villages which came in its way. (Page 118)[9]

Shah Jahan gave orders to plunder the mahalls of Galna and Patora during the Ahmadnagar campaign. (Page 136)[10]

During the Bijapur Campaign, the Imperial Army of Shah Jahan pillaged the town and slaughtered the population of Gulbarga. (Page 156)[11]

Note- In Court chronicles and Jadunath Sarkar books there is mention of destruction of Kulbarga, I believe that it's the same city with a different name but still can't be 100% sure.[12,13]

B.P. Saksena states that when the imperial army had to retreat back out of the Bijapur Siege, the army started to commit wanton outrages on the inhabitants of Bijapur. On their way back they enslaved women and children, sabotaged and pillaged every town that came in their way. (Page 158- 159)[14]

Another religious intolerance and bigotry step taken by Shah Jahan was that he ordered the abolition of Shi'ism(Shiaism) religion in the Golconda country. (Page 174)[15]

During the Badakhshan campaign, the Imperial Army after plundering the frontier districts returned to Kabul. (Page 192)[16]

The Imperial Army also despoiled some districts of Kandahar and Bist during its siege. (Page 227)[17]

Neighbouring districts of Bist were also plundered. (Page 234)[18]

The working class and peasantry were brutally oppressed and the increment in revenue from 1/3 to 1/2 of the total produce made it even worse. (Page 292)[19]

Other religious intolerance and bigotry steps taken by Shah Jahan were that he didn't allow people of other religions to wear the dress code of his state religion. Furthermore, he prohibited the adherents of other religions to bury or burn their loved ones near the graveyards of the followers of his state religion. Moreover, he also created a whole new department for the conversion of people belonging to the other religions to his state religion. (Page 294-295)[21]

INFORMATION FROM VARIOUS ARTICLES ON INTERNET

I was able to gather some more data regarding the other cruelties, religious intolerance steps, and policies made by Shah Jahan from a couple of scholar (research) and history articles on the Internet. Before moving further, I want to clarify one aspect regarding the information taken from these articles and web pages found on the Internet as per my personal experience. The details regarding Shah Jahan which I have taken from the books written by Jadunath Sarkar, V.A. Smith, B.P. Saksena, and Henry Miers Elliot can be easily found in the articles available on the Internet (not all the information that has been mentioned above but some main points of it). Moreover, those articles and research pages were the only reason through which I was able to learn about the books and research of Jadunath Sarkar, V.A. Smith, B.P. Saksena, and H.M. Elliot regarding Shah Jahan and his reign.

I went on to read those books from which the information has been taken for the articles. I did it to double check and to clear my doubt that the authors of those articles are not making things up, creating fictional quotes and points by themselves and then referring to a 100-year-old book and also a historian who existed like 100 years ago. But whatever quotes and facts that those articles stated have been taken from the books were true. I was able to find all the quotes and other points the same as mentioned in those books. From here one point can be proven which is that those articles are authentic, the authors and the writers of these articles are not being biased or making up things by themselves for a particular reason (I am not saying that the information mentioned is 100% valid but I would personally put the accuracy of the particulars mentioned at 96%). That's the reason why I have also included some more details and cruelties done by Shah Jahan taken from these articles into my book. The informative material from those articles is mentioned below:

HINDU PRINCESSES- Shah Jahan did not marry any princesses of other religions, unlike his father and grandfather who married princesses of other religions.[1,2] From here, it can be said that the environment of his harem and court started to shift towards his state religion because there were no princesses or other influential persons in his seraglio who belonged to other religions (except for the old princesses of Akbar or Jahangir if they were alive).[1]

K.S. Lal in his book The Mughal Harem gives us the number of Rajput princesses from the reign of Akbar to the reign of Aurangzeb. Akbar had 33 Rajput princesses in his harem while Jahangir had 7, Shah Jahan had only 5, while Aurangzeb had 9. Jahangir had 7 Rajput wives (as per mentioned by Xavier and Blochmann) while Akbar had 12 - 17 Rajput wives.[2] I was not able to find or mention of any Rajput princess who was married to Shah Jahan. The 5 Rajput princesses probably could have been married to the other royal members or princes of Shah Jahan's mughal empire. During the reign of Akbar, maybe Jahangir also, the Rajput princesses were allowed to follow and practise their religion but with the accession of Shah Jahan and his religious intolerant policy, there came a drastic change.[2] First Shah Jahan did not have any interfaith marriages but even if he had, then the Rajput princesses were first converted and made to accept his state religion before getting married to any prince of the mughal empire. It can be easily proven from the fact that when Anup Kunwar, daughter of Amar Singh was about to get married to Prince Sulaiman Shukoh, Shah Jahan himself taught her to recite kalima and she was converted to his state religion before getting married (Lal, 1988).[2]

Note- In another paragraph, K.S. Lal claims that Akbar had no less than 38 Rajput princesses among which 17 were married to Prince Salim (Jahangir), it is a little confusing but still, it doesn't affect anything regarding the point which I am trying to make.[3]

JIZYA TAX- Shah Jahan reintroduced the unjustified Jizya Tax (some sources claim that he reintroduced the pilgrimage tax, not jizya but even the pilgrimage tax is also similar to that of jizya tax) which is a type of tax which had to be imposed on and paid by the people belonging to other religions other than the state religion of Shah Jahan. The lower class and the middle-class citizens belonging to other religions were already facing injustices and oppression at the hands of Shah Jahan, and the imposition of the Jizya Tax made it even worse. This religious intolerant step didn't last for too long as Shah Jahan had to remit this unjustified tax. It was made possible by a deputation led by a Benares scholar Kavindaracarya against this new tax rule in Shah Jahan's court.[4]

Other religious intolerance and bigotry steps taken by Shah Jahan were that he stopped the celebration of festivals of other religions in his court and in the 7th year of his reign, Shah Jahan ordered that followers of other religions who will accept his state religion are allowed to get their full share of property from their father.[5]

Dr. A.L. Srivastava in his book The Mughul Empire quotes regarding Shah Jahan, his religious fanaticism and the corruption in his reign as *"His religious bigotry and intolerance anticipated the reactionary reign of Aurangzeb. He forbade repairing of the old Hindu temples as also the building of the new temples... His persecution of heretics in Islam made the Shias feel that they were unwelcome at the imperial court. His fondness for money impelled him to increase the burden of the people and caused suffering among them. His love of presents accorded sanction to a pernicious custom of gilded bribery. The offering of nazars and presents became common not only at the royal court and camp, but also in the households of imperial nobles and officers and became responsible for a great deal of corruption in administration. His display of pomp and magnificence resulted in extorting money from the unwilling masses and classes, and his sensual tastes set a bad standard of public and private morality* (Srivastava, 1986, p. 326)." [6,7]

Furthermore, in a not so popular opinion, Dr. A.L. Srivastava also states that Mumtaz Mahal orthodox views could have contributed to Shah Jahan's harsh policy of religious fanaticism.[6]

GOLDEN AGE OF THE MUGHAL EMPIRE

From the writings of notable and authentic historiographers like Jadunath Sarkar and V.A. Smith who have done a lot of hard work and extensive research on their books. Also from the well-researched books of Fergus Nicoll, B.P. Saksena, Ricardo Mcgee, and various other articles, the claims of Shah Jahan being a merciless tyrant and cruel emperor gets even stronger. As these books are well researched and based on original sources, all the facts and information regarding Shah Jahan and his reign shown in these books will be true (especially for the Jadunath Sarkar, B.P. Saksena, and V.A. Smith ones followed by Fergus Nicoll). From written records, it can be easily concluded that the reign of Shah Jahan was not the Golden Age for the working class. The golden reign of Shah Jahan proved to be a curse for the working class and peasantry, the working class was brutally oppressed, tortured, and abused by the ruthless policies and methods adopted by Shah Jahan and his corrupted administration to extract revenue from them, to attack, plunder, ravage their homes, and conquer their independent kingdoms.

Various religious intolerant steps, slave trade, and confinement of prisoners of war were openly practised and Shah Jahan legalised those inhumane practices. Shah Jahan totally reversed the religious tolerant policy set by his grandfather Akbar by introducing Jizya Tax (or pilgrim tax). Both of these taxes were banned by Akbar in 1563 (Pilgrim Tax) and 1564 (Jizya Tax).[1,2] Also, Shah Jahan legalised the slave trade which was abolished by Akbar in 1562 and capturing of POWs which was illegalised by Akbar in 1563.[3,4] Shah Jahan was not a liberator like his grandfather Akbar, he was an oppressor like his son Aurangzeb.* Alternatively, it can also be said that Aurangzeb became an oppressor and a fanatic because of his father Shah Jahan. But still, people are gonna be like it was the Golden Age mainly because of the stupendous mughal architecture. Dr. A. L. Srivastava also makes a similar point.[5] All the magnificent, extraordinary, dazzling monuments, and sumptuous buildings which were built during this 'golden age' and which represented the enormous wealth, art, and riches of the Shah Jahan were nothing other than a byproduct of barbaric plundering.

*Note- The author has compared these three Mughal Emperors. The author isn't trying to condone various iniquitous crimes and wicked deeds perpetrated by Akbar during his reign.

These majestic monuments were laid on the foundations of abuse and ill treatment of the kind, innocent hard working citizens of India. These monuments and symbols of love like the ugly Taj Mahal, other architectural buildings, and enormous wealth were made and created with the blood of benignant civilians. The wealth which these monuments represent was nothing other than the plundered and stolen stuff from the deserving working class. The love which these monuments represent is nothing other than a disguise which has helped these despicable wretches to hide their abuse of power, authority, and hate beneath it.

For sure, it was the Golden Age for the abusers, for the corrupt, for the tyrannous administration and officials of Shah Jahan, and for the oppressor himself who loves to spread hate and ruthlessness with the power being directed at them.

For sure, it was the Golden Age for the heavily morally decayed Imperial Army whose sole purpose throughout its entire existence was to commit massacres, ravage, attack, and loot everything that comes in its way; the same army which loved to spread chaos, terror, and injustice among the people who were just trying to defend their homes and save their lives, their honour of themselves and their wives, their daughters, their mothers, their children from the perverted eyes of the emperor, his satanic administration or his morally decayed army.

For sure it was the Golden Age for the emperor himself, for the Shah Jahan who loved lustful activities and loved having those activities during his entire life, for the potentate who loved to spread tyranny, for the autarch who loved the oppression, abuse, and misery of the working class.

It was a Golden Age for the emperor who built his entire empire through countless massacres and gruesome barbarities, who collected vast fortunes and made a peacock throne out of that wealth with the help of ruthless marauding and oppression of the weak, the hardworking, and the deserving souls.

For sure it was the Golden Age for all of these despicable wretches and tyrants including Shah Jahan who were able to get away with all of the war crimes and dreadful misdeeds that they did as nobody questioned them and they were never brought to justice. All of these pathetic swines lived a happy and prosperous life at the expense of the working class. It was not the golden age for the courteous and the innocent, it was the abusive era of the mughal reign for them. The so-called Golden Age was a hoax, a lie, and always has been.

Before moving further, let's understand the concept of words like war crimes, crimes against humanity, and genocides. And also, what type of deeds or activities that are committed by the individual or the army during times of war or any kind of other event like revolts, protests, etc. are considered to be war crimes, crimes against humanity, and genocide.

Chapter 6

War Crimes, Crimes Against Humanity, and Genocide

WAR CRIMES

According to Article 8 of the Rome Statute of the International Criminal Court, an act is considered to be a war crime if any of the following actions were committed during the times of war.[1]

Paragraph 2

A. Grave breaches of the Geneva Conventions of 12 August 1949, namely, any of the following acts against persons or property protected under the provisions of the relevant Geneva Convention:

    i.   Wilful killing

    ii.   Torture or inhuman treatment, including biological experiments;

    iii.   Wilfully causing great suffering, or serious injury to body or health;

    iv.   Extensive destruction and appropriation of property, not justified by military necessity and carried out unlawfully and wantonly;

    v.   Compelling a prisoner of war or other protected person to serve in the forces of a hostile Power;

    vi.   Wilfully depriving a prisoner of war or other protected person of the rights of fair and regular trial;

    vii.   Unlawful deportation or transfer or unlawful confinement;

    viii.   Taking of hostages.

B. Other serious violations of the laws and customs applicable in international armed conflict, within the established framework of international law, namely, any of the following acts:

i. Intentionally directing attacks against the civilian population as such or against individual civilians not taking direct part in hostilities;

ii. Intentionally directing attacks against civilian objects, that is, objects which are not military objectives;

iii. Intentionally directing attacks against personnel, installations, material, units or vehicles involved in a humanitarian assistance or peacekeeping mission in accordance with the Charter of the United Nations, as long as they are entitled to the protection given to civilians or civilian objects under the international law of armed conflict;

iv. Intentionally launching an attack in the knowledge that such attack will cause incidental loss of life or injury to civilians or damage to civilian objects or widespread, long-term and severe damage to the natural environment which would be clearly excessive in relation to the concrete and direct overall military advantage anticipated;

v. Attacking or bombarding, by whatever means, towns, villages, dwellings or buildings which are undefended and which are not military objectives;

vi. Killing or wounding a combatant who, having laid down his arms or having no longer means of defence, has surrendered at discretion;

vii. Making improper use of a flag of truce, of the flag or of the military insignia and uniform of the enemy or of the United Nations, as well as of the distinctive emblems of the Geneva Conventions, resulting in death or serious personal injury;

viii. The transfer, directly or indirectly, by the Occupying Power of parts of its own civilian population into the territory it occupies, or the deportation or transfer of all or parts of the population of the occupied territory within or outside this territory;

ix. Intentionally directing attacks against buildings dedicated to religion, education, art, science or charitable purposes, historic monuments, hospitals and places where the sick and wounded are collected, provided they are not military objectives;

x. Subjecting persons who are in the power of an adverse party to physical mutilation or to medical or scientific experiments of any kind which are neither justified by the medical, dental or hospital treatment of the person concerned nor carried out in his or her interest, and which cause death to or seriously endanger the health of such person or persons;

xi. Killing or wounding treacherously individuals belonging to the hostile nation or army;

xii. Declaring that no quarter will be given;

xiii. Destroying or seizing the enemy's property unless such destruction or seizure be imperatively demanded by the necessities of war;

xiv. Declaring abolished, suspended or inadmissible in a court of law the rights and actions of the nationals of the hostile party;

xv. Compelling the nationals of the hostile party to take part in the operations of war directed against their own country, even if they were in the belligerent's service before the commencement of the war;

xvi. Pillaging a town or place, even when taken by assault;

xvii. Employing poison or poisoned weapons;

xviii. Employing asphyxiating, poisonous or other gases, and all analogous liquids, materials or devices;

xix. Employing bullets which expand or flatten easily in the human body, such as bullets with a hard envelope which does not entirely cover the core or is pierced with incisions;

xx. Employing weapons, projectiles and material and methods of warfare which are of a nature to cause superfluous injury or unnecessary suffering or which are inherently indiscriminate in violation of the international law of armed conflict, provided that such weapons, projectiles and material and methods of warfare are the subject of a comprehensive prohibition and are included in an annex to this Statute, by an amendment in accordance with the relevant provisions set forth in articles 121 and 123;

xxi. Committing outrages upon personal dignity, in particular humiliating and degrading treatment;

xxii. Committing rape, sexual slavery, enforced prostitution, forced pregnancy, as defined in article 7, paragraph 2 (f), enforced sterilization, or any other form of sexual violence also constituting a grave breach of the Geneva Conventions;

xxiii. Utilizing the presence of a civilian or other protected person to render certain points, areas or military forces immune from military operations;

xxiv. Intentionally directing attacks against buildings, material, medical units and transport, and personnel using the distinctive emblems of the Geneva Conventions in conformity with international law;

xxv. Intentionally using starvation of civilians as a method of warfare by depriving them of objects indispensable to their survival, including wilfully impeding relief supplies as provided for under the Geneva Conventions;

xxvi. Conscripting or enlisting children under the age of fifteen years into the national armed forces or using them to participate actively in hostilities.

C. In the case of an armed conflict not of an international character, serious violations of article 3 common to the four Geneva Conventions of 12 August 1949, namely, any of the following acts committed against persons taking no active part in the hostilities, including members of armed forces who have laid down their arms and those placed hors de combat by sickness, wounds, detention, or any other cause:

i. Violence to life and person, in particular murder of all kinds, mutilation, cruel treatment, and torture;

ii. Committing outrages upon personal dignity, in particular, humiliating and degrading treatment;

iii. Taking of hostages;

iv. The passing of sentences and the carrying out of executions without previous judgement pronounced by a regularly constituted court, affording all judicial guarantees which are generally recognized as indispensable.

D. Paragraph 2 (c) applies to armed conflicts, not of an international character, and thus does not apply to situations of internal disturbances and tensions, such as riots, isolated and sporadic acts of violence, or other acts of a similar nature.

E. Other serious violations of the laws and customs applicable in armed conflicts not of an international character, within the established framework of international law, namely, any of the following acts:

i. Ordering the displacement of the civilian population for reasons related to the conflict, unless the security of the civilians involved or imperative military reasons so demand;

ii. Killing or wounding treacherously a combatant adversary;

iii. Destroying or seizing the property of an adversary unless such destruction or seizure be imperatively demanded by the necessities of the conflict;

Paragraph 3- Nothing in paragraph 2 (c) and (e) shall affect the responsibility of a Government to maintain or re-establish law and order in the State or to defend the unity and territorial integrity of the State, by all legitimate means.

CRIMES AGAINST HUMANITY

According to Article 7 of the Rome Statute of the International Criminal Court, crime against humanity means any of the following acts when committed as part of a widespread or systematic attack directed against any civilian population, with knowledge of the attack:[2]

i. Murder;

ii. Extermination;

iii. Enslavement;

iv. Deportation or forcible transfer of population;

v. Imprisonment or other severe deprivation of physical liberty in violation of fundamental rules of international law;

vi. Torture;

vii. Rape, sexual slavery, enforced prostitution, forced pregnancy, enforced sterilization, or any other form of sexual violence of comparable gravity;

viii. Persecution against any identifiable group or collectivity on political, racial, national, ethnic, cultural, religious, gender as defined in paragraph 3, or other grounds that are universally recognized as impermissible under international law, in connection with any act referred to in this paragraph or any crime within the jurisdiction of the Court;

 ix. Enforced disappearance of persons;

 x. The crime of apartheid;

 xi. Other inhumane acts of a similar character intentionally causing great suffering, or serious injury to body or to mental or physical health.

GENOCIDE

According to the Article II of the Convention on the prevention and punishment of the *Crime of Genocide*, genocide means any of the following acts committed with intent to destroy, in whole or in part, a national, ethnical, racial, or religious group as such:[3]

 i. Killing members of the group;

 ii. Causing serious bodily or mental harm to members of the group;

 iii. Deliberately inflicting on the group conditions of life calculated to bring about its physical destruction in whole or in part;

 iv. Imposing measures intended to prevent births within the group;

 v. Forcibly transferring children of the group to another group.

Source- United Nations Office on Genocide Prevention and The Responsibilty to Protect

SUMMARY

Now, if you look at the acts which define war crimes, crimes against humanity, and genocide and compare them with the events that had been taken from the text of official court chronicles of Shah Jahan's reign, it can be easily said that Shah Jahan and the Imperial Army which worked under his jurisdiction committed various horrific war crimes, crimes against humanity, and amoral genocides on the people of India. Basically, he did each and everything, there wasn't even a single thing or a point in the definition of genocide and crimes against humanity which he didn't did. Along with that, he and his Imperial Army committed around 85% of all activities that defined war crimes. The only acts which the pitiless Shah Jahan didn't perform included things like attacks on humanitarian assistance personnel and stuff provided by the UN or using emblems of Geneva Conventions or UN. The other deeds which he didn't commit were using poisonous gases or biological weapons, or augmented bullets. Logically, UN humanitarian aid or Geneva Convention emblems, augmented bullets or biological weapons didn't even exist during the era of Shah Jahan's reign. That's why Shah Jahan didn't commit those acts, if those things existed and available to him during his reign, then for sure he and his army could have used them to carry out various other disgraceful acts. Because Shah Jahan and his army both lacked moralities and basic human values. Indirectly, it can be said that he could have easily executed all of the acts that define war crimes if he was using modern weapon technology. This is a speculation which can be easily proven with the help of the evidence taken from the past. I have listed the activities that happened during Shah Jahan's reign in the definitions of war crimes, crimes against humanity, and genocide to make it easier for you to understand and compare those acts with the text of court chronicles mentioned in chapter 4. From here it can be easily concluded that Shah Jahan didn't become the wealthiest emperor, instead he became the wealthiest war criminal during his reign.

Moreover, from the books of Jadunath Sarkar, V.A. Smith, B.P. Saksena, Fergus Nicoll, Ricardo Mcgee, and many Internet Articles, the accusations of Shah Jahan committing numerous war crimes, genocide, and crimes against humanity get even stronger, valid and authentic. From the information mentioned in previous chapter 5, we were able to get more details regarding several disgraceful and horrific deeds perpetrated by

Shah Jahan and his administration. Those heinous acts, events, or incidents which were not mentioned or found in the court chronicles.

Note- India is not a member of the ICC (International Criminal Court) but India is a member of the UN. And all member nations of the UN automatically become members of the ICJ (International Court of Justice) aka the World Court which is the main judiciary body of the UN. Both the ICJ and ICC accept and follow the same definitions and guidelines for war crimes, crimes against humanity, and genocide.[4,5]

Chapter 7

Six Fundamental Rights

Hindustan, presently known as the Republic of India and is the world's biggest democracy. The constitution of India not only mentions six fundamental rights but it guarantees those six fundamental rights to every citizen of India. Theoretically and practically, it is impossible for any individual, any government official, or any judiciary body either the District/Local Court, High Court, or the Supreme Court to deny or take away those six basic rights from the ordinary citizens of India. The only exception as per Article 21 is to the citizens found guilty of any crime or illegal activity which basically includes people who are criminals, terrorists, rapists, murderers, etc.[1] Those Six Fundamental Rights are as follows:[2]

1. THE RIGHT TO EQUALITY

2. THE RIGHT TO FREEDOM

3. THE RIGHT AGAINST EXPLOITATION

4. THE RIGHT TO FREEDOM OF RELIGION

5. CULTURAL AND EDUCATIONAL RIGHTS

6. THE RIGHT TO CONSTITUTIONAL REMEDIES

Now, Among these six basic rights, Shah Jahan being the Emperor of India (even though he didn't rule or conquered all of India but whatever land he ruled was a part of India except for Afghanistan) failed horribly at providing and guaranteeing these basic rights to the common citizens of India. Instead, he was the one who took these rights away from the citizens of India. He was the one who stole these rights away from the common citizens of India. He took away the right to equality by imposing special and heavy taxes, and religious intolerance policies on citizens belonging to other religions than the state religion. He took away the right to freedom by owning slaves, taking prisoners of war and putting them in confinement and treating them with great cruelty and misery, destroying and ravaging the homes of countless hardworking citizens during his war campaigns, forcibly throwing the peasantry and working class into the slave trade. He also compelled these helpless people to sell their women, and their children as slaves to the officials and rich elites of his state religion if the peasantry was not able to pay the unjustified high land revenue imposed on them. He and his corrupt administration took away the Right against Exploitation from the common citizens of India because they were the ones who were exploiting the working class.

The poor, miserable conditions and ill- treatment of the working class at the hands of Shah Jahan and his corrupt administration for their own greedy and undying needs have already been mentioned in the Jadunath Sarkar and the V.A. Smith books, especially the latter. Fergus Nicoll, Ricardo Mcgee, and even B.P. Saksena also mentions the misery and abuse of the working class and peasantry during the reign of Shah Jahan in their books. He and his commanders exploited the women in the harem, also captured and took women hostages during their war campaigns as trophies to make them their lust toys and sex slaves. He took away the Right to Freedom of Religion and basically all cultural rights by sabotaging places and violating statues belonging to other religions and cultures. Along with that, he also didn't provide the right to constitutional remedies as he was the one who was taking away all those rights. Shah Jahan was never a protector or a saviour but he was the arch nemesis of people, their rights, and their lives.

Shah Jahan also failed to provide the Right to Life as he and his army killed and massacred countless ordinary people. Furthermore, he also took the Right to Property by invading and conquering lands; despoiling and ruining properties belonging to the citizens of his own empire or the sovereign states. These people had earned those things and wealth with honesty, hard work, and determination, not like the tyrannous policies of plundering, corruption, injustice, and cruelty followed by Shah Jahan and his administration to build their piles of wealth and extend their reign of terror, oppressiveness, and abusiveness in all corners of the country.

Now, maybe some of you could have started to wonder why the author is accusing Shah Jahan of taking away the Fundamental Rights from the Citizens of India even though these rights didn't come into effect until the 26th January 1950 when the constitution of India was implemented.[3] Shah Jahan and his reign were gone for 350 years by that time. Presently, it's been over 400 years since Shah Jahan's era. The simple answer is that these rights were not new, these rights were always there even though they were not recognized but they were there. That's one of the reasons why Shah Jahan had to spend his entire life fighting war campaigns against the independent kingdoms of India. That's the reason why he faced so much resistance and revolts from the independent realms. Because he didn't only try to ransack and conquer their lands but he was also taking away their rights, their freedom, their culture, their religion, and everything else. Even during those times, people had these rights, they knew these rights and they fought for those rights. They deserved those rights. So stating that the six fundamental rights were not present, made, or implemented during Shah Jahan's reign is totally incorrect. Therefore, Shah Jahan should not be blamed and charged for taking those rights away from the citizens of India is totally incorrect and false. None of those rights were created or made by the Constitution of India. But still, one point can be stated i.e. the Constitution was the first legal body that gave those rights a proper name, a word, or an organised structure by distinguishing these rights and putting them into specific categories. The only thing that the constitution of Independent India did was the documentation, legislation, and implementation of those rights. It made every citizen of India aware of these rights in an organised, civilised, and easier way. Those rights were always there since the foundation of the entire human civilisation.

Moreover, Shah Jahan should also be blamed for killing humanism, morality, and basic human etiquettes in the imperial army. He was the one who was responsible for the moral decay of the Imperial Army. His Imperial Army did not follow any basic rules and regulations related to moral values and humanism during times of war. As the entire reign of Shah Jahan was full of wars and revolts, the Imperial Army which was fighting all these wars didn't have any code of conduct and restrictions which could have prevented it from committing various war crimes and atrocities. There are lots of events in the court chronicles where it states how the imperial army used to ravage lands, destroy and pillage property, and whatever thing that comes in its way. Also, the army did not spare the guiltless ordinary citizens of the enemy state or we can say the citizens of India. It was not the imperial army that was doing it all by itself but it was the Shah Jahan, his commanding officers, or the princes who used to give orders to the Imperial Army to commit these wicked crimes on the sovereign lands. Shah Jahan for sure was aware of these severe malfeasances and barbaric acts being carried out by the imperial army but he failed to take any action regarding it which could have prevented the imperial army from perpetrating these genocides and massacres. Shah Jahan could have saved the countless lives of innocent hard toiling citizens but he didn't. It seems like he loved to watch innocents suffering in pain and dying in agony. It feels like the countless lives of soft-hearted, hard-working citizens were not considered worthy enough of being saved and protected, those lives didn't mattered enough to Shah Jahan, his sons, his officers, and his monstrous Imperial Army.

Chapter 8

Political Integration Of India

Shah Jahan just like his ancestors wanted to conquer all of the Indian subcontinent. But he didn't wanted to win India by having peaceful conversations and negotiations with the independent dominions of India during that time. If he had followed this step then he could have been able to make those independent states join the Mughal Empire and unite all of India under his regime. He could have never promised anything like religious tolerance policies and equal treatment towards all beliefs and religions. He could have never talked about cultural appropriation and equal rights for all citizens. If he had promised these things and adopted these policies, then it could have helped him in gaining the trust of the rulers as well as the citizens of those Independent kingdoms and those states could have joined his reign happily and peacefully. In this way, lots of meaningless wars and revolts could have been prevented. In this way, countless lives could have been saved from getting killed unnecessarily and without any cause. But he didn't do it as it looks like he didn't wanted to do it. It seems like he never tried to choose this path because he didn't had any sympathy for the citizens of his empire. Instead, Shah Jahan tried to impose and force his extremist views, beliefs, and his religion on the native population of those independent states mainly because of his ego, arrogance, and haughtiness. He went onto the path of cruelty, injustice, hate, and oppression to conquer India just like his ancestors. His arrogance, his abomination, his mercilessness, his hunger for power, and his greed cost the lives of millions of affectionate civilians who had nothing to do with it. Many of the independent domains who fought and revolted against the Shah Jahan's Reign of Hate were nothing in size compared to the size of his empire and the imperial army. Most of these realms were just small forts or towns but still, the people of those lands were willing to die fighting instead of just surrendering to the tyranny of Shah

Jahan. They didn't want to become a part of the hateful empire ruled by a fanatic. From here, it can be easily concluded that the citizens of India were losing their rights and freedom under Shah Jahan's reign of terror and that's what compelled them to keep on fighting and resisting the ruthless emperor till the very end. If Shah Jahan wanted to be a true emperor, if he really thought that he was the only king that the people of India needed, he was the only ruler that India deserved, then he should have tried to win over the hearts of the people of India with love, kindness, and empathy. But he didn't seem to have words like politeness and love in his dictionary, he only wanted to rule and conquer all of India. It looks like he had a mentality that made him believe that India was his birthright given to him by his ancestors. Just like his ancestors who were invaders, he also started to do the same, he started to invade and conquer the self governing territories of India. He tried to conquer India with hate and oppression. Shah Jahan became the sole reason behind the brutal massacre of the peace and harmony of this beautiful nation during his reign.

We can easily compare Shah Jahan's greed for expanding his empire and ruling over the entire India with the Political Integration of India that happened after India got separated from the British Empire and became an independent country in 1947. This political integration wasn't done via waging wars on the independent states to make them join India. The goal of a United India was achieved with the help of peaceful conversations and negotiations. The demands and conditions set up by the princely states were also being heard and accepted. Those princely territories were given options to either join India or Pakistan or even to remain Independent. Those states were not forced in any way to join India. Sardar Vallabhbhai Patel aka Iron Man of India who was the Deputy Prime Minister of India during that time was given the responsibility of making those princely kingdoms join India.[1] Finally, under his leadership, guidance, and great negotiation and conversational ability, 562 princely states decided to become a part of India.[2] Those 562 princely realms joined India happily without any revolt or war. The main reason behind it was the various rights that the citizens of those princely states will receive if they become a part of India. Rights like religious tolerance, equality, cultural and language acceptance, gender equality, democracy, and many more things like these helped the monarchs, and people of those princely states to have their faith and trust that will make them join India. From here, it can be easily concluded that Shah Jahan tried to make the many independent states to become a part of the mughal empire with hate, power, and oppression without guaranteeing those independent nations any rights, which led to innumerable brutal wars and bloodbaths causing the countless lives of innocents. Basically, Shah Jahan became the wealthiest tormentor during his reign. That's the reason why Shah Jahan failed terribly at uniting those self governing-states with his empire. The political integration of India was a total success as it was totally opposite to Shah Jahan's approach of terror, hate, and harsh ransacking. Today, the Republic of India is a union of 28 States and 8 union territories.[3]

Chapter 9

The Workers of the Taj

The Taj Mahal was built in approximately 21-22 years (1631 - 1653).[1] Around 20,000 workers were employed to build the Taj Mahal. As Peter Mundy quotes regarding the Taj Mahal construction *"It goes on with excessive labour and cost"*.[2] Those 20,000 diligent, hard working people gave 20 years of their life and hard work to build a monument for a wretched tyrant. According to a legend, it is said that after the completion of the Taj Mahal, Shah Jahan ordered the cutting off of both the hands of the 20,000 workers. 20,000 hard-working labourers who spent years working day and night to build the grotesque Taj Mahal finally got recognition from Shah Jahan. The appreciation that those innocent labourers got was in the form of the mutilation of their hands. The reason given behind such a wicked act was that Shah Jahan was afraid of the thought that somebody else will also be able to build a magnificent and sumptuous dome like the Taj Mahal with the help of the same labourers who built the original Taj Mahal. So, in a way to prevent this possibility, to stop it from happening anywhere in the future, Shah Jahan decided to cut off the hands of these labourers. It is still considered a myth or a lie because there are no official records or documentation available regarding this from the past. Several historians have said that there is no evidence to prove this myth, to prove that it actually happened. Also, some historians claim that those workers could have been put into some kind of a contract which could have prevented them from working with any other king or building any other similar mausoleum like the Taj Mahal.[3,4] But just like the myth itself, there isn't any record or document from the past which can be used to prove this point or opinion too. Also, whatever information we have regarding Shah Jahan is mostly taken from his court chronicles. As I have said earlier, these official document records had been entirely funded and monitored by Shah Jahan and his administration. We are only reading and knowing about those events and things which Shah Jahan wanted us to know. We are not reading those court chronicles through our eyes, and understanding those records through our own perception, we are reading those court chronicles through Shah Jahan's eyes and maybe even understanding through his perception. If we read and understand these court chronicles through his point of view, then why should he like to keep a record of chopping off the hands of 20,000 innocent workers? Nobody in the world, even a king or an ordinary individual, had ever wanted to have a negative image or to receive hate from future generations. Everybody wants to be loved, respected, adored, and treated as a nice human being, Shah Jahan also wanted the same. That's the reason why his court chronicles never mention anything regarding the condition of women and girl slaves in the harem, those records never tell us anything regarding the life of slaves in the imperial army as well as the entire empire, there is no mention of the living conditions of the ordinary citizens of Shah Jahan's empire in his official histories. There isn't any mention of any workers who built the Taj Mahal, I mean people who actually worked on the project, not the architects or the designers. I am talking about the working class, daily wage workers. I will not be amazed even if Shah Jahan ordered the chopping off of the hands of the workers who built the Taj Mahal to maintain the beauty of the fugly Taj Mahal. As he already committed a lot of heinous crimes and atrocities, his court chronicles literally states that. He and his army were already morally decayed, so it wouldn't be a big deal for him to do the same with these poor hard working peasants. If it happened, then that incident has been whitewashed from the history of his reign, the history of India and the world. I am not saying that I am 100% sure it happened but there is a 50%-50% possibility of it happening or not.

Moreover, everybody says that the Taj Mahal was built by Shah Jahan which is not true. People are just saying it because that's what Shah Jahan had wanted to hear. He wanted to be remembered as the builder of the Taj Mahal because that was the only good thing which he did during his entire reign. I mean that's what he had thought about while building the Taj Mahal. In reality, the Taj Mahal was built by 20,000 hard toiled daily wage workers. The unknown, the nameless 20,000 individuals who had laboriously worked day and night to build it. Those individuals could have been overworked and severely underpaid without receiving any overtime pay. Because there were no labour boards and labour laws back in the day to protect these labourers from exploitation and to make them aware of their rights. Workers who had given 20 years of their life to built a monument for a hateful emperor, a dictatorial potentate who was morally decayed. Those innocent hardworking people couldn't have seen their families for years, and had to work under miserable working conditions and survive under poor living circumstances. The daily wage labourers could always have been treated like shit based on their religion, caste, or social status. But still, their hard work, dedication, and pain can be seen on the walls and floors of the ugly Taj Mahal. Sadly, none of those people, the individuals who actually built the Taj Mahal had been named. It feels like their names have been erased from history. They had been robbed of their hard work, their determination, their passion, and maybe even their happiness. Their appreciation, names, and recognition had been stolen by Shah Jahan in the same way he stole and pillaged the houses, peace, rights, equality, and justice from the citizens of India. He brutally ransacked and decimated everything that could have helped us to build a better India and a better world.

Chapter 10

The Butterfly Effect

DEFINITION AND EXPLICATION

Edward Norton Lorenz was an American mathematician, meteorologist, and the author of the Butterfly Effect.[1] He stated that the non-linear equations that govern the weather have such an incredible sensitivity to initial conditions, that a butterfly flapping its wings in Brazil could set off a tornado in Texas.[2] This statement was a scientific definition and understanding of the Butterfly Effect.

However, The Butterfly Effect can also be applied to human behaviour and character, their actions, and the consequences caused by those actions. A small action can lead to a big consequence. And those consequences will take effect within minutes, days, months, years, or even centuries. All of us are connected in one way or the other. A small act of compassion anywhere in the world will make us happy and it will make us show how beautiful this world is as there is still goodness and kindness present in it. On the other hand, an act of abhorrence will make us angry and feel broken. That anger can easily turn into hate and that hate can turn into a much more violent thing. We learn from the mistakes which we did or from the horrendous blunders executed by mankind in the past. Sometimes we fail to learn from our mistakes as well as the mistakes of humankind. We try to forget our past or the heinous past of human civilisation. In some circumstances, we are made to forget the past while in some we deliberately do it. Sometimes some events of the past or history have been altered or entirely whitewashed to change our views and perceptions regarding some prominent individuals or any historical event. Having a different view and approach to something which was entirely based on a lie and that lie which we believe was the truth can cause serious damage to the people, society, and the entirety of human civilisation. Mainly the rich and the powerful were able to alter history because of their wealth, influence, and power. And it's a well-known fact that most rulers of the past were evil, cruel, and full of contempt. They had used their powers to oppress the poor, the weak, the hardworking, or anybody who stood against their tyranny. The same pathetic individuals have also used their power to alter history and they have tried to erase many atrocities and inhuman acts which they had committed from the pages of history. They tried to rewrite history in their favour, to make them look great, and to be treated and worshipped like gods. As lies don't last forever, most of those scorned swines have gotten hate from future generations for the things that they did in the past. But still, some of them were able to get away with it, they succeeded in whitewashing history and altering it in their own favours. Shah Jahan was one of those wretched people. A tyrant who is seen as a true lover, Romeo of India and his shrine of lies aka Taj Mahal is being worshipped as a symbol of love but in reality, he was a worthless bandit who became the wealthiest thief in India. How his whitewashing and alteration of the history of India has caused serious injury to the country and the whole world. An injury that is getting worse with every passing day. As we are all connected and related to each other due to which all of us are affected and hit by the crimes of Shah Jahan may be directly or indirectly. That's what the butterfly effect really is. I will try to explain it by pulling and connecting many strings of the past and historical events that have shaped modern India in the upcoming paragraphs.

Just like cultures, heritages, and languages are passed from generation to generation. Similarly, various social skills, basic human values, kindness, and love are also passed from generation to generation, from one culture to another culture. In the same way, hate and evil are also being passed from generation to generation, from time to time. In my opinion, the only reason why hate is being passed on from one generation to the next generation is that individuals, or sometimes the entire society fail to understand the difference between hate and love, war and peace. Human psychology, thoughts, and nature work in such a way that every individual believes that whatever they are doing is right. For some people, their actions could be a symbol of love and justice while for others those actions may represent hate and injustice. It mainly depends upon individual perception and thinking. In my opinion, one of the ways to find out whether our actions are good or bad is to always put ourselves in the position of those who will be affected or influenced by those actions. Moreover, while taking any action we should always obey and act in accordance with various laws and regulations set up by the judiciary bodies. Here is an example of what I am trying to say; Let's consider that you are a drug smuggler and drugs are illegal in your country. Before selling drugs to a drug addict, you thought that you will make some quick money by selling this drug which will help you to live a better and more comfortable life (this is kind of an example of selfish behaviour and negative/unlawful use of the individual freedom which has been granted to you via democracy). Along with that, you also put yourself under the shoes of that drug addict and you are like I am a drug addict now and I will love this brand new drug that will take me to heaven and give wings to my imagination. You sell that drug to that drug addict. First of all, you committed a crime by selling an illegal drug, and secondly, you also worsened the mental and physical health condition of that drug addict by giving him more drugs. He will become a burden on his family as well as on society unless he is able to get rid of his drug addiction. In this way, you will also become a criminal and a threat to society. So, always keep these things in mind while taking any action.

We as humans have always been more attracted to and affected by negative things. We get more focused on negativity. Hate and evil are one of those negative things. Nowadays, social media, news outlets, and the internet play a major role in giving attention to these things. For example- among thousands of acts of tenderness, love, and positivity, only 1 of those good deeds would be able to make news headlines or start trending on social media platforms. On the other hand, it takes only 1 act of hate to make it a hot topic for discussions and debates on various news outlets, social media platforms, and the whole internet. That one incident of monstrosity and negativity can reach the entire nation and the entire world within minutes of media coverage. That coverage can influence people in a good way or a bad way but for sure it will have an impact. The same thing cannot be said for kindness and positivity. I am not saying that acts of hate and injustice getting too much attention is bad. The best and hopeful thing about acts of hate and unlawful nature getting more attention is that there will be more awareness among the general public and society about it. Society will try to find the reasons behind it and also it will try to fix the mistakes and issues causing it. Moreover, people will also fight and protest to bring the culprits to justice who were responsible for spreading hate and chaos. Nowadays, even children are becoming aware of it, they are able to differentiate between what's right and what's wrong, what's considered to be hate and love. Most of the individuals responsible for spreading hate all around the world have been brought to courts and justice. But the sad part is that even after so much awareness, hate is still out there, it is still devouring our beautiful world. That hate hits us hard every time we hear about it, every time we see it even though it is happening in another corner of the world. Whenever we see it, hear about it or feel it, we feel unsafe and defenceless.

Also, I still can't fully understand why we love to idolise criminals and gangsters, why our singers and many influential people promote gun culture, and the things and activities which are deemed to be unlawful, illegal, and responsible for the moral degradation of humanity. And if any of these well known individuals, mainly rappers, die due to gun violence, gang war, or due to drug overdose, they are honoured by giving the title of being legends by their blind and brainwashed followers or fans. I don't know why we love to make and watch songs on gun culture or a movie based on the life of a gangster or a drug smuggler. The idealisation of these filthy criminals is done by the working class and also the working class is the one who has to suffer and lose their lives and freedom at the hands of these worthless criminals and gangsters. In my opinion, the main reason behind this issue is that we fail to understand the consequences of such glamorization. And also we fail to differentiate what's right and what's wrong. The idolisation and glorification of hateful tyrants like Shah Jahan has to be stopped not only because we have to serve justice and avenge the innocents who had to suffer at the hands of these ugly swines. But also to save our kids, vulnerable members of society who lack intellectual thinking from idolising the ideologies of these wicked individuals which will eventually destroy their humanism and cause their moral depravity. That moral degeneration will make them commit various felonies and disgraceful acts and they will try to justify those horrific deeds by comparing those actions to the acts and legacy of tyrants like Shah Jahan. At last, they will become criminals and a burden on society and a curse to the civilised world. That's how criminals are made, they idolise somebody i.e. youngsters idolise gangsters and drug smugglers due to influence of social media and the glamorization of gun culture by society, singers, moviemakers etc. who welcome these uncivilised wretches and makes their abhorrent manoeuvres look cool.

Nobody knew when or from where the hate came from. But one thing is for sure, it was not there during the birth of the human race. That's the reason why a baby always has a smile on his/her face. You can see their eyes sparkling with kindness and their hearts beating with love. Abhorrent things like hate, injustice, violence, etc. don't even exist in their dictionaries. But while growing up, they were affected by society. They get to know about love, hate, discrimination, and many terrible things like this, and they were impacted by it. Typically, how they were raised, how they were treated by their parents and society also plays a major role in it. Due to this, some of them get attracted to the dark side, towards hatred and wickedness, and they start to get morally decayed. Their eyes get filled with hate while their heart gets devoured by sinister darkness. But still, many of them were able to remain generous and loving throughout their lives. In the end, love binds us while hate splatters us. This world still exists, not because of hate but because of love and kindness. Because there are more good people who spread love and tenderness as compared to the bad ones who spread hate and chaos.

Have you ever wondered why Babur invaded India and started forcing his religion on the people of India back in the 16th century? Why were the Mughal Emperors barbaric and merciless autarchs? Why did Shah Jahan destroy religious places belonging to other religions? Why does he have a harem despite Mumtaz being his true love? Why did his son Aurangzeb turn out to be a religious fanatic? Why was India separated into two nations entirely based on religion? Why was there a Hindu-Muslim-Sikh massacre during the 1947 partition of India? Why there was a brutal genocide and ethnic cleansing of Kashmiri Pandits happened in the 1990's Kashmir? Why were there anti-Hindu-Muslim riots in Gujarat in 2002? Why were there terrorist attacks in Mumbai and Ahmedabad in 2008? Why were there the 2013 Muzaffarnagar riots? Why was there another riot in the capital city of India in 2020? Why were there so many incidents of communal hate that have happened in these past years? Why women are still victims of domestic violence, torture, oppression, and rape in India? Why Polygamy is still legal in India even though in all of the developed countries and some Muslim majority countries too, it's illegal? Why does the caste system still exist in India? And many more malicious things like this are still prevailing in India as well as the entire world. These things full of hatred and moral degeneracy have been infecting and destroying mankind for centuries. It's all the butterfly effect.

CONNECTIONS

Babul was the first mughal emperor of India and he was the one who started the mughal dynasty in India. He was the 5th descendant of Timur from his father's side and from his mother's side he was the descendant of Genghis Khan.[3,4] Both of these individuals are considered the biggest, most brutal, and worst mass murderers in the history of entire human civilisation as we know it. Genghis Khan who formed the Mongol Empire was known as the biggest mass murderer of all time. According to an estimate provided by several historians, he viciously man slaughtered around 40 million civilians during his various war campaigns which could have equal to 11% of entire world's population.[5] On top of that he had sexual relations with so many women, to be precise he raped so many women that currently, around 0.5% or 16 million male inhabitants of Earth are related to Genghis Khan.[6] Timur was also a ruthless killer just like the ferocious Genghis khan. He was a Turco-Mongol conqueror and the founder of the Timurid Empire.[7] He killed an estimated 5% of the total world population during his reign. It is equal to around 17 million innocent souls.[7] He was extremely intolerant towards other religions. That was one of the reasons why he invaded India in 1398 because he believed that the Sultans of Delhi were extremely tolerant to non-believers and were allowing people to follow and worship other religions.[8,9] It is estimated that Timur's army slaughtered around 50,000 - 100,000 inhabitants of Delhi and took another 100,000 as slaves.[9] Following in the footsteps of his descendants, Babur carried out the same horrific atrocities and genocides on the citizens of India. In 1526, after invading and capturing Delhi, Babur massacred and killed innumerable innocent citizens belonging to other religions.[10] Moreover, with great pride and without any kind of shame or guilt, he mentions it in his official memoir BABURNAMA.[10]

Just out of extreme rage and anger, Akbar who was the grandson of Babur and the grandfather of Shah Jahan also committed the heinous crime of slaying 30,000 of the country's people who took part in defence during the Siege of Chitor (1567-1568).[11] Moreover, Akbar also ordered to bury his favourite concubine Anarkali aka Nadira Begum alive in 1599.[12] He did it out of suspicion and jealousy of her being in a relationship with his son Salim (Jahangir).[12] There were also other incidents in which Akbar committed various cruelties out of rage. In the history books of India and also the whole world, Akbar is considered great, not just because of his name but also because he has been compared to his Mughal ancestors and descendants. He could have been less cruel than his ancestors and descendants but it doesn't mean he should be given the title of BEING GREAT.[13] The renowned historian V. A. Smith has said that all the mughal emperors, even Akbar who in fact were Timur descendants, were Asiatic Despots.[14] Human life didn't matter enough to them and all of them were capable of ordering ferocious massacres and cruel punishments.[14]

Jahangir was the father of Shah Jahan and the next Mughal emperor after Akbar. He was an alcoholic and he had around 300-400 women which included his wives and concubines in his harem.[15,16] Jahangir blinded his own son Khusrau who rebelled against him. He also ordered the brutal killing of 200 - 300 of his son's followers by hanging them on trees or impaling them on stakes.[17,18] Once Jahangir with great cruelty started beating a nobleman to his death because the nobleman accidentally broke his favourite china dish.[19] Jahangir was gonna kill him if he wasn't stopped by the prince.[19] Now, just like his ancestors, Shah Jahan also did the same. Basically, he was trying to save the legacy of his ancestors, grandfather, and father. I have already mentioned all the heinous abominations and vicious acts done by Shah Jahan in the previous chapters. Shah Jahan also committed acts of fratricides by killing his half-brother Prince Khusrau in 1622 and ordered the murder of all of his male relatives in a bid to secure the Mughal throne after the death of Jahangir in 1627.[20,21] Also, Shah Jahan rebelled against his father Jahangir.[22] As I have stated earlier that just like love and kindness, hate is also being passed from generation to generation. The Mughal dynasty is the best example of it. That hate doesn't stop with Shah Jahan. After Shah Jahan, his son Aurangzeb followed in the same footsteps as his father and his ancestors.

It is a well-known fact that parents play a major role in the overall personality and moral development of their children from their early childhood days. Every kid tries to copy the actions of their mom and dad. That's the only reason why culture, heritage, and languages are being passed from generation to generation. Because before getting influenced by society, children get influenced by their parents. Even after becoming adults, they are still influenced by them. So, it becomes the sole responsibility of their parents to teach their kids about moral values, humanism, and the difference between right and wrong. Parents should never set a bad example for their kids. For example - if the parents are doing drugs or any illegal activity in front of their kids, then for sure the kids will try to do the same as they have seen their parents doing it. One thing is for sure, the mughals were not being considered to be good parents. All of them were cruel, merciless, mass murderers, perverts, and full of hate. Shah Jahan who is considered as the Romeo of India, a true lover, and a benevolent emperor failed horribly at setting a good example of being a good parent and a benignant human being in front of his kids. He failed to teach his kids the difference between what's right and what's wrong. He failed to protect his kids from evil, instead, he was the one who threw them onto the path of wickedness. He failed to teach Aurangzeb basic human values and moralities, the language of love and tolerance, the seed of peace and harmony, and the smell of the air that comes with freedom, justice, and equality. Shah Jahan didn't teach him anything other than hate, bigotry, cruelty, injustice, undying greed asking for more and more, and every other nefarious thing that could have been existing in his pitiless mind. Shah Jahan became one of the biggest reasons behind the moral degradation of Aurangzeb.

Following in the footsteps of his father or we can say learning from his father Aurangzeb (November 3, 1618 - February 21, 1707) went on to revolt against his father Shah Jahan and he sent Shah Jahan to prison for the rest of his remaining life i.e. from 1658 - 1666.[23,24,25] Moreover, he also perpetrated acts of fratricides by killing his brothers Dara Shukoh (Aurangzeb's theologians proved Dara to be an apostate and he was killed on 30th August 1659) and Murad Baksh (beheaded on 14th December 1661) to take the mughal throne during the war of succession.[26,73] He also got his nephew

Sulaiman Shukoh (the son of Dara Shukoh) killed in 1662.[27] Furthermore, Aurangzeb blamed Shah Jahan for the civil war and he also accused Shah Jahan of depriving him of any paternal love and showing partiality by giving Dara all the love, importance, and power.[28] He also blamed Shah Jahan for causing hate among the 4 brothers.[28] He went on to become the cruellest mughal emperor in the history of the entire mughal dynasty. In fact, he broke down all the records of atrocities, mercilessness, inequities, and religious bigotry. He followed the policy of 100% religious intolerance. For him, every man, woman, and child belonging to different religions, other than his state religion, were infidels (kafirs). He didn't even spare the followers of his own religion i.e. followers of Shia Islam.[29] It is estimated that during the reign of Aurangzeb around 4.6 million innocents were murdered and slaughtered, which puts Auangzeb among the top 100 most cruel and atrocious despots to ever live on the pages of history.[30] Carrying with him enormous hate, ruthlessness, and uncounted war crimes, he was able to expand the mughal empire to its greatest length. Wherever he and his army went, that place got sunken into an ocean of blood and chaos. His cruelty and hate broke down all the boundaries and walls of humanity, and basic moral values. In fact, he was so cruel, his hate was so enormous, his crimes were so horrifying, and he was so morally decayed that to stop him, Guru Gobind Singh (1666 - 1708) aka The 10th guru (saint) of the sikh faith had to become vigilant.[31] In a bid to stop his tyranny and end his reign of terror and harsh policies of repression, Guru Gobind Singh had to go onto the path of violence. (The militarisation of Sikhism was started after Shah Jahan's father Jahangir brutally tortured to death the 5th Guru of Sikhs Guru Arjun Dev).[32] It doesn't mean that the gurus did not try to stop him with non-violence and peaceful negotiations. The 9th guru of sikhs aka Guru Tegh Bahadur (1621 - 1675) was executed by Aurangzeb in 1675 after he failed to make the guru accept his state religion.[33] Guru Tegh Bahadur sacrificed himself to save the dignity and lives of Kashmiri Pandits who were facing untold inhumanities and forceful conversions at the hands of this religious bigot. Guru Tegh Bahadur was also the father of Guru Gobind Singh. Choosing the path of vigilance wasn't the only option, it was the only option that was left behind after trying everything else. Just imagine what kind of a despicable wretch and barbaric monster Aurangzeb could be that a saint has to become vigilant. Sikhism was founded in the 15th century by Guru Nanak Dev (1469 - 1539).[34] Sikhism was formed as a means to end various social prejudices, injustices, and caste systems and to promote women's equality in the Indian Subcontinent. In 1705, a Zafarnama (epistle of victory) was written by Guru Gobind Singh and it was sent to Aurangzeb.[35,36] Aurangzeb broke the oath that he took on the holy quran by allowing his army to attack Guru Gobind Singh and his followers while they were marching out of the Anandpur Sahib Fort.[35] The letter told Aurangzeb that he believes he is a true follower of his religion but he is the one who broke all the beliefs and oaths of his own religion.[37] He is the one who disrespected his own religion and god.[37] That letter made Aurangzeb question his own religious beliefs, legacy, and faith. After reading the Zafarnama, Aurangzeb finally had guilt and remorse. Out of his guilt, he ordered all of the imperial army to never attack the Sikhs.[38] He even calls himself a sinner in one of the letters which he had written to his son during the last years of his life.[38, 39]

After the death of Aurangzeb (i.e. 1707), the mughal empire finally started to shrink and slowly fade away into dust. Thanks to the contributions of Guru Gobind Singh of Punjab and Chhatrapati Shivaji Maharaj (1630 - 1680) and Marathas of the Maratha Empire who led several revolts against the tyrant Aurangzeb.[40] Both individuals stood for justice, liberty, religious tolerance, and equality. The last of the mughal emperors were nothing other than being puppets of the new power that was rising in India i.e. The British Empire represented by the East India Company.[41] Various historians have said that the Britishers followed the policy of divide and rule which helped them to rule over India over the next 100 years. In my opinion, it were the mughal emperors who were responsible for this policy with a minor difference that was hate, divide, and rule. They propagated so much hate and discrimination on the basis of religion during their reigns that the Indian society already started to scatter and crumble. The British only reorganised their policy of hate, divide, and rule into divide and rule. (It was true that Indian society was already scattered by the caste system but the policy of religious fanaticism and persecution adopted by the mughal potentates made it even worse and stronger). Everything was already done by the Mughals, the British just improvised it. The British were also able to take advantage of the injustices and outrageous atrocities committed by the Mughals as a means of weapon to build trust within the people of India that had helped them in making the Indian-subcontinent their colony. V.A. Smith has also mentioned a similar point.[42] Emperors like Shah Jahan also didn't properly try to end various social malpractices and superstitions like the sati pratha in Indian society as the practice was still allowed to perform by his corrupted administration. Along with that, the Mughals totally ignored the issue of the caste system in India because all of their focus was on the extreme policies of religious intolerance, abuse, pillaging, and war campaigns with independent states to expand their oppressive empire. Due to their negligence towards the caste system, it still exists in modern India in the 21st century. The caste system is just like racism. Along with that, the merciless tyrants like Shah Jahan didn't invest or focus on scientific experiments, medical research, technological advances, and modernisation of India. During all my research, all the books, and articles that I have read related to the reign of Shah Jahan, I was not able to find even a single mention of any investment or fund which he had contributed for research on these fields which could have helped in the advancement and progress of the Indian society and entirety of human civilisation. He should have at least invested in the medical research and experimentation that could have helped save the lives of countless women as his own wife Mumtaz died due to a pregnancy issue. Also, he could have invested in this sector in a bid to discover the causes and preventive measures for the famines which were making the already miserable lives of the poor people of his empire even worse. He could have done it in honour of his wife if he really loved her, remembered her, or cared about her but he didn't. But he squandered around 10 million rupees on his peacock throne, 5 million rupees on the Taj Mahal, and on several other monuments and edifices. He also lavished millions on the monthly salaries, and allowances of his sons, daughters, and other members of the royal family, on his luxurious lifestyle and needless war campaigns. The investments in these types of things did not serve any purpose other than to fulfil the arrogance, boast the ego and keep the worthless achievements of this ferocious monster alive. These dazzling monuments and buildings didn't help the working class but the development of these exorbitant monuments and vile thrones burden the already burdened working class. Because all the money used to build these shrines of lies has to be paid by the working class in the form of revenues and that's one of the reasons why revenues increased during Shah Jahan's reign. The monuments and shrines of lies built by these wicked tyrants serve no purpose and have contributed nothing to the working class, nature, technological advancements, and modernisation of human civilisation. These monuments only represent oppression, hate, and abuse. These monuments and shrines of lies are no good for society and never were.

In my opinion, one of the reasons why tyrants like Shah Jahan were religious fanatics was because of the misinterpretation of the text written in their holy books. But due to their misinterpretation, India got infected with the poison of hate that is still hurting and haunting the people of India for centuries now. It wasn't just hate, it was the disease of religious extremism that these despicable wretches brought with them. The disease which now feels like it will stay here forever until the end and it will keep on devouring India as well as the entire mankind for centuries to come. After the mughal era was gone, the next biggest massacre that ever happened in India was during its partition in 1947. The main reason behind it was the volcano of religious hatred that was built by mughal period emperors like Shah Jahan. India was divided into two nations based on religion. Partition came at a great price as there was a bloodbath among the people of different religions. It was mainly the Hindu-Sikh vs the Muslims. Around 1 - 2 million innocent souls lost their lives in the communal and religious riots that happened in the states of Punjab and Bengal.[43] The partition built an unbreakable wall of hate between the two nations. That's why India and Pakistan have fought over 4 wars since the partition. The volcano of religious fanaticism again erupted in the 1990s when Kashmiri pandits had to face another genocide since the Mughals left them. In 2002 that volcano of religious loathe again erupted in the form of Hindu-Muslim riots in Gujarat. Mumbai and Ahmedabad attacks were also a byproduct of partition and religious extremism. In 2013 it again erupted in Muzaffarnagar. In 2020 the same happened in the capital city of India, New Delhi. The disease of religious extremism hasn't just remained limited to the state religion of these pathetic wretches but that disease has spread to other religions too making it a highly communicable infection that is slowly degrading the moralities and etiquettes of the society. Currently, the volcano of communal and religious hatred has been active since the past few years causing various religious riots, spreading communal hate and propaganda. Whenever that volcano of religious hate erupted, poor guiltless and hardworking people had to suffer, they had to lose their rights, their freedom, their lives, and the lives of their loved ones.

WOMEN RIGHTS

POLYGAMY- Polygamy is the practice or custom of having more than one wife or husband at the same time.[44] In India, Polygamy is legal for Muslim individuals and some tribal communities.[45] Polygamy is illegal in all developed and western countries which even includes some muslim majority countries like Turkey and Tunisia.[45] Personally, I don't have any problems with polygamy, if you view it as some kind of an open relationship. The issue that I have with the legalisation of polygamy in India is that it's not the polygamy which is legal, it is *polygyny* which has been made legal. Polygyny is a form of polygamy in which a man has more than one wife.[46] In India, Muslim men can marry up to 4 women while on the opposite side, women can only marry 1 man. One point is to be made here which is that polygamy among muslims is declining every decade and it can be proved from the 1961 Census Survey of India in which it was founded that only 5.7% of Muslims were living in polygamous relationships.[47] This number decreased by more than half in 2005-2006 India's National Family Health Survey in which it was found that only 2.5% of muslims were living in polygamous marriages.[47] In the latest NFHS Survey of 2019-2020, this figure further declined to 1.9%.[48] This declining trend also applies to other communities too.[47,48] We can also take a look at big muslim superstars of India who never had any polygamous marriages. The conclusion which can be derived from here is that polygamy isn't even that popular or it is practised widely so there is no need to keep it legal. Legalisation of polygamy just represents one thing and ideology which is a curse to women as well as the entire society. It is that the legalisation of polygamy represents a patriarchal society in which women are considered inferior or less equal to men. Polygamy not only represents but it causes the birth of the patriarchal society, and it basically works as a breeding ground for patriarchy. The worth and life of 1 man is equal to the worth and life of 4 women. The founder of BMMA (Bharatiya Muslim Mahila Andolan) has said that Polygamy is "abhorrent - morally, socially and legally".[47] UN Human rights committee has said that polygamy violates the dignity of women and it should be abolished.[47,49] Polygamy should not only be banned but it should be criminalised in India as soon as possible just like the Instant Triple Talaq (Divorce). If it is not banned and criminalised then the other method that can be adopted is that the rules of polygamy should be amended to make the practice legalised equal for both the genders just like in an open relationship.

RAPE CASES- In 2020 alone, there were 28046 cases of rape reported in India. It implies that during that year, on average around 76-77 women were being raped every day.[50] Also, if we take a look at the average of the last 11 years i.e. 2010-2020, 85 women had been raped daily in India.[50]

DOMESTIC VIOLENCE- As per the research study by BMC Women Health, between 2001 and 2018, there has been a 53% increase in cases of domestic violence against women.[51] 1,548,548 total cases were filed during this time period and around 35.8% (554481) of these domestic violence cases were filed between 2014-2018.[51] Also, another point that is to be noted here is that these numbers are just based on the number of cases that have been filed in the police station, there could have been more cases of rape and domestic violence that are not reported. Also, sometimes victims of domestic violence don't even report these incidents because of family or societal pressure and fear of retaliation. This number could be double or even triple these numbers as there are still regions in India that are pretty much backward and very less developed. In those regions, the chances of a woman becoming a victim of these kinds of crimes increase due to a lack of awareness among women regarding their rights. Also, the presence of a patriarchal society in those regions makes it even worse than the rest.

Another surprising study by the National Family Health Survey 2021 has revealed that an average of over 30% of females from 14 states believe that it is totally acceptable for husbands to beat and torture their wives under certain conditions.[52] This percentage goes up to 80% of women that are fine with their husbands being violent towards their wives in 2 states (Telangana and Andhra Pradesh) out of 18 states where the survey was conducted.[52,53] This is the another shocking survey which easily proves that the patriachal society is still present and acceptable in India. The main reason behind the presence of a patriarchal society in India is the oppression, misery, and abuse of women. There is no doubt that back in the old times, women were considered inferior to men in the entire world. But with time, western world started treating women equally. But in India, it didn't happen on a large scale. As merciless invaders started to invade India, the condition of women became even worse. During the invasions, men were slaughtered and their wives, and daughters were taken away as trophies. They were being raped and molested. The women were just treated as sex slaves, pleasuring tools or child bearing machines, mughal emperors were also invaders and they also treated the women of India just like the other predatory marauders. Their harems were the best proof of this tyranny and abuse. I had already mentioned about numerous scandals and incidents related to lust and licentious nature of Shah Jahan and the harem. Moreover, in his court chronicles, it had already been mentioned whenever there was a war campaign and the enemy was about to lose the campaign, they surrendered themselves so that they could be able to save the honour of their women and the captured females were also being sent to the harem. It happened for centuries and generations of women were affected by it. Prolonged oppression, torture, rape, and molestation of women in India, led to the formation of a patriarchal ideology and society that still exists in 21st century India. That's the reason why polygamy is still legal in India, women are becoming victims of rape and domestic violence daily. Due to the prolonged oppression, the ideology of Indian women has already been affected, that's why at least 30% of women justified domestic violence. Because the women have been made to believe that the men are superior to them and they are their property. Mughal emperors like Shah Jahan should also be blamed for this as they didn't do anything to uplift the status of women in society. With the enormous wealth, power, and influence that these people had, they could have easily done it without facing much criticism and resistance but they didn't. Mainly because tyrant Shah Jahan was not a protector but an abuser. He was the abuser of women's rights and liberties. The patriarchal society could have ended in India by the 21st century if these wicked people could have taken aggressive steps that had focused on towards the upliftment of women in Indian society.

ISLAMOPHOBIA

It is the negative belief and prejudice towards Muslims or Islam by people belonging to other religions. Some individuals are scared of muslims or islam while others dislike muslims. That dislike or fear turns into hate towards the Muslims. Today, In India Islamophobia is increasing day by day. Barbaric tyrants like Shah Jahan are responsible for this. People who are Islamophobic believe that if muslims become the majority or islam becomes a powerful religion in India then the devotees of other religions again have to face oppression, religious persecution, and discrimination. Their fear of losing their rights and religion is directly linked to the past and by past, I mean the actions of the barbarous potentates like Shah Jahan. Basically, mughal emperors like Shah Jahan chose a state religion and secularism wasn't even a word that existed in their tiny wretched brains. Then, the adherents of other religions who didn't follow the state religion became victims of oppression and forceful religious conversions. It kept on happening not only for years but for entire centuries because every mughal sovereign did it. All the mughal emperors followed the same state religion including Shah Jahan. The religion they selected to be the state religion was Islam and which is why we have Islamophobia. Some of them were heavy drinkers like Jahangir and wine was one of the popular drinks in their seraglios.[54,55] Shah Jahan drank wine when he turned 24 years old (in 1616) and after that on some other occasion he made a promise to never drank wine again but he broke that promise at a later time.*[56] Even Aurangzeb drank wine just to impress his favourite concubine Hira Bai (aka Zainabadi).[57] Wine is prohibited in Islam.[58] Akbar was accused of blasphemy as he forbade public prayers, Ramazan fast, and the Mecca pilgrimage.[59] Also, during his reign mosques were turned into stables and no new mosques were built or repair of the old mosques was prohibited.[59,60] And many more regulations like this even question the religious tolerant policy of Akbar as he had tried to prohibit or stop practices of his own religion.[59,60] Once Jahangir with a burst of mocking laughter disregarded the blasphemous claims of Nakib Khan (he was a history student who used to read histories to Akbar) and told him to bury the issue.⁶¹ The main reason behind those claims was that the Jahangir had allowed the priests to denounce Muhammad as a false god and the language used by priests regarding the Prophet was considered to be blasphemous by Nakib Khan.⁶¹ Also, dancing and music are discouraged in Islam but still Shah Jahan used to enjoy dancing girls.⁶²,⁶³ Even in his confinement, he was provided with plenty of dancing girls along with his entire harem.⁶³ Moreover, despots like Aurangzeb used to break oaths that they took on their holy book.⁶⁵,⁶⁶ Both Shah Jahan and Aurangzeb were hostile towards followers of Shia Islam (probably considered them to be infidels or heretics).⁶⁷ On top of that Shah Jahan also used to attack muslim kings who have their own sovereign kingdoms such as Abdullah Kutb Shah (or Qutb Shah), ruler of the Golconda Kingdom and he even compelled them to recite khutba under his name.⁶⁴ Dreadful tyrants like Shah Jahan or Aurangzeb were both usurpers and autocratic in nature, this was the only reason why they became the emperor and stayed in power. These tyrants were able to justify and cover their usurpercy and autocracy under the blanket of theocracy. That's one of the reasons why the mughal empire is considered a theocratic state. The point that can be concluded from here is that these contemptible dictators weren't even true followers of their religion and its core beliefs. From here, it can be easily said that these pathetic swines used religion only as a shield or a cover to justify various wicked deeds and atrocious acts which they committed against the populace of India. If these tyrants had chosen Hinduism as the state religion, then in today's world we would have been hearing the word Hinduphobia. If these scumbags had chosen Sikhism, Christianity, or Buddhism etc. as the state religion, then there would have been Sikhphobia, Christianophobia, or Buddhaphobia trending in these present times. You see, it isn't religion, it was these monstrous monarchs like Shah Jahan who were responsible for the birth of religious phobia. No matter which religion they choose to be the state religion, followers of other religions had to face oppression, abuse, religious discrimination, and persecution due to the malicious, arrogant, and egoist nature of these tyrants.

*Note- B.P. Saksena doesn't provide any details regarding the future incident when Shah Jahan breaks his promise to never touch wine again. Moreover, Fergus Nicoll claims that Shah Jahan made a public declaration to never touch alcohol and wine again in the year 1621.[68,69]

CORRUPTION

India is infected with the worms of corruption. Corruption is one of the biggest obstacles in the technological advances and modernisation of India and also the whole world. Mainly all the developing and under-developed countries have higher levels of corruption as compared to the developed nations. As per the 2021 Corruption Report surveyed by Transparency International Organisation, India ranked 85 out of 180 Countries with a CPI (Corruption Perceptions Index) score of 40/100.[70] The lower the CPI score, the more corrupt the country is.[70] India's CPI has remained steady since 2016.[70] The disease of corruption is not new in India, it's been here for centuries. Corruption was also there in the mughal dynasty, there was mention of presence of corruption during the Reign of Akbar.[71] Corruption was one of the reasons why the peasants and middle-class people were so much oppressed and ill-treated during Shah Jahan's reign. Mughal Emperors did little to nothing to stop this evil. Even though they tried to end crime with cruel and pitiless methods of justice but that cruel justice was just meant for the petty thieves, criminals, local revenue collectors, peasants, etc. That cruel justice never went on to grab the necks of the cruel and corrupt top officials and powerful members of the Empire. I can give you some examples of it and one is during the reign of Shah Jahan, the governor of Mughal Deccan Khan-i-Dauran brutally tortured and abused the peasantry and working class in a bid to extract more revenue from them.[72] Shah Jahan knew about it but he didn't even give him a warning to not do it again and serving the cruel and true justice was a far away thing. He was able to get away with it because of his higher post and authority. Moreover, Shah Jahan had also shown partiality while dealing with disputes involving people of different religions with the followers of his state religion. Due to this, devotees of other religions and beliefs hesitated to approach Shah Jahan's court mainly because out of fear of retaliation.[73] Another example which can be given here is of his father Jahangir who was also known as to provide cruel justice and was barbarically tyrannical but still he was lenient and partial when the cases of official corruption came to his court. In one such occasion, Jahangir ordered to shave the head of an imperial officer who was accused of taking bribes while being stationed at the river Ravi in Lahore.[74] But if the same thing was done by a peasant (which in reality could have never happened), he (Shah Jahan or Jahangir) could have mercilessly and brutally slaughtered him in front of his court. It is one of the reasons why corruption is still prevalent in India due to lack of awareness, weakness, and partiality in anti-corruption laws among the rich, the poor, the powerful and the weak. The rich and powerful individuals were able to easily save themselves from these laws. Also, the poorly implemented anti-corruption laws (laws that do not even spare the rich, powerful, and highly influential individuals) makes it even worse.

From here, it can be easily concluded that whatever religious problems, communal hate and women's safety issues, and even somehow corruption that India is facing today, mughal despots like Shah Jahan are to be held accountable for it. They are linked to these issues directly or indirectly due to the butterfly effect. The amount of hate, abuse, injustice, and discrimination spread by pitiless tyrants like Shah Jahan is still out there in present times and it can be easily observed happening around us. These despicable wretches did not keep their moral degradation to themselves, instead, they spread that moral degeneration, or their moral depravity was passed onto their children, their followers, and the whole society. The various incidents of communal hate, religious extremism, and violence that had happened in these past few years show the moral deterioration of Indian Society. The problem is not about moral degradation as entire societies, nations, and the entirety of human civilisation has been suffered, ruined, and consumed by this disease throughout the veins of time as it is not new, it has been there since the foundations of human race. The real problem is it's not going away, the moral degeneration of the society is getting worse day by day. This disease of moral degradation will spread everywhere, in every corner of the world if it's not stopped or a cure for it is not found. Everybody, no matter where you live or die will be affected and suffered by it as every human in this world is linked and connected to each other either by globalisation or by the butterfly effect.

CHAPTER 11

CONCLUSION

Before moving further, I want to clear a doubt or a question that could have been arising in your mind. That question could be why the author is just hating and criticising Shah Jahan even though there were other Mughal emperors, kings, and invaders who were much crueller and committed worse heinous misdeeds on people of India and the whole world. Why is the author just targeting Shah Jahan; he isn't even the worst of all? The simple answer to this question is that every other mughal despot, king or invader has been treated as a tyrant. They have been viewed as criminals, mass murderers, symbols of cruelty, hate, and injustice. Every Indian and the whole world detests them for the crimes and atrocities which they had done during their lifetime. But for Shah Jahan, this viewpoint has been totally opposite from the rest. Shah Jahan has been admired throughout history, he has been treated as a great emperor and a loving human being, he has been viewed as a true lover by the historians, the people as well as by the school books that are read by children in India and maybe even the whole world. Yes, he could have done some good deeds but just from those few good deeds, the entire character and portrayal of Shah Jahan shouldn't be made. Sadly, that's what the historians did, they drew the entire personality and character of Shah Jahan by just keeping in mind those few good deeds while totally rejecting and ignoring the atrocious and dark past of Shah Jahan. They basically made it look like it didn't happen or even existed. Those horrific wrongdoings and brutal outrages don't matter enough or were not considered worthy enough to be added to their works. The number of vicious crimes which he perpetrated were more than the number of good deeds which he did. Shah Jahan proudly mentions those few good deeds along with his wicked acts (the inhuman deeds which seemed righteous to him) in his court chronicles for his own glorification and the rest of the exaltation is done by the historians and other prominent individuals of the society. But in reality, all of it was a lie and always has been a lie. We have been fed up with that lie from our childhood. We have been listening to that lie from our birth till our death and that's why that lie has become the truth for us.

From all of the facts in the chapters mentioned above, it can be easily proven that Shah Jahan was a merciless tyrant just like the rest of the mughal emperors. He was not a lover but a hater. The only thing that he ever love was hate. He was not the wealthiest emperor but he was the richest raider of the world. He failed to build and maintain peace and harmony in his empire as he spent most of his years waging wars with the neighbouring kingdoms, he failed to expand and unite his empire with the independent states through peaceful negotiations and meetings, and he failed to provide even basic rights to the citizens of his empire, instead, he was one who took it all away from them. He failed to take good care of his wife Mumtaz Mahal, his true love. He failed to understand the mental and physical health condition of his wife who was getting pregnant every year. He failed to provide any rights to the women of his nation, he failed to protect their self-respect and their dignity. Instead, he was the one who was depriving those women of their honour, he was the one who was taking away their dignity and honour by having hundreds of concubines and women slaves in his harem. He and his commanders treated those women as their libido toys, child-bearing machines, and statues of lust. He failed to end various social prejudices and practices that were oppressing women during his reign like the sati practice. He failed to build moralities and basic human values in the Imperial Army. He failed to question and stop the various heinous acts executed by the imperial army during the war campaigns and he was the one who allowed the imperial army to commit those inhuman deeds. Due to this the Imperial Army committed multiple acts of war crimes and crimes against humanity. He was responsible for the moral decay of the Imperial Army. He failed to end the caste system, in fact, he made it even stronger as he never even

Conclusion

tried to look into matters of the caste system. Whatever officials and high rank commanders of other religions he had in his administration, most of them belonged to the Rajput community and this community is considered an upper caste. I was not able to find any mention or information regarding the presence of a high-ranking official who belonged to a lower caste or a tribal community in the administration of Shah Jahan. Even if they were present, then still those individuals could not have gotten importance or the same treatment as the members of the royal castes like Rajputs had received during that time.

This point can be easily proven as the Rajput generals and commanders have been mentioned in great detail regarding their lives and ranks in all of the historical books that I have read so far related to the reign of Shah Jahan but nothing is mentioned related to the other communities, probably the individuals of the lower castes and the tribal communities. (Note - All the assumptions and opinions made on the caste system, the Rajputs, and the tribal communities have been made by considering the old caste system of the old times. By old times, I mean the mediaeval times when the caste system was at its peak. I have not made these opinions on the condition of the present-day caste system which is not that much aggressive, and it is not followed and accepted by a large portion of the population of India today as compared to the older times.) There is one more point that also needs to be made over here regarding the army commanders of other religions who were employed in the imperial army of Shah Jahan. All of them have gotten lower ranks as compared to the generals who were the followers of the state religion of Shah Jahan.[1] These commanders were also morally degraded just like Shah Jahan and his imperial army. They supported the religious intolerant policies of Shah Jahan even though those policies were attacking and harassing their own religions.

On top of that commanders like Raja Debi Singh even participated in activities which involved the demolition of religious places belonging to his own religion (Saksena, 1932).[2] The names of these generals which represent their particular religions were more of a formality, a kind of show-off other than being a necessity to follow, stand, and fight for their own religions and rights. They were not to be considered true blood of Rajputs or other communities who have their own honour, dignity, and ethics.

Shah Jahan failed to be a good parent to his children and he failed to teach them about basic human values like justice, equality, peace, and harmony. He failed to set himself up as a good example for his kids. He himself didn't understand the difference between what's good or bad, right or wrong. He failed to understand the true meaning of the holy quran. Shah Jahan failed as a son, as a father, as a husband, and worst of all he failed as an emperor for his people. He didn't achieve anything, he didn't have any glorious and magnificent accomplishments. Predominantly, Shah Jahan failed at everything except for the achievements that he ever accomplished were basically failures.

He was worse but not less than Adolf Hitler, the remorseless dictator of Nazi Germany who committed the holocaust of Jews during World War 2. Germany had gotten only one Hitler but India got a dozen more wretches like Hitler including Shah Jahan. But still, Hilter was brought to justice and he had to pay for the crimes and cruelties that he committed during his lifetime. He wasn't glorified or venerated after his death, the only thing he received was hatred from the public and society. But, in the case of Shah Jahan, it was the total opposite. The treatment Shah Jahan received after his death was totally contrasting from other barbaric despots like Adolf Hitler. Shah Jahan has been glorified, idealised, and idolised by historians, common people, children, and society. The Taj Mahal has worked like a blanket or a sort of cover under which all the heinous crimes and the dark past of Shah Jahan has been kept hidden. Nobody even tried to unfold that blanket. Even though that blanket was unfolded several times as most of the information regarding the life and atrocities of Shah Jahan has been documented in his official autobiographies and various other historical books.

Conclusion

Also, many historians have criticised Shah Jahan in their writings. Some people knew it but still, nobody ever tried to question it. Nobody ever tried to ask why a tyrant has been glorified and his shrine of lies has been worshipped as a symbol of love. It feels like after uncovering the blanket of bitter truth, it was again put into hiding under the cloak of the Taj Mahal. Evil was allowed to survive, hate was allowed to live, and injustice was allowed to rise. That's why there is still wickedness present in this world which is hurting innocent and hardworking individuals. Injustice and hate are spreading chaos and terror among the weak, poor, kind, and helpless souls. Evil and barbarism have been used by the powerful, merciless tyrants, and mass murderers like Shah Jahan to spread sufferings, endure pain among the lower class, soldiery, daily wage workers, peasants, and labourers. It is also happening in the present times. The rich and the powerful are still using hate and various ferocious methods to oppress the weak and the ordinary people.

The world was not built by the kings and the politicians but it was built by the working class. Sadly, it was also the working class that had to suffer the most. The emperors or the politicians love to wage wars but they never fought those wars. Those wars are fought and won at the expense of the soldiers of the working class. Whenever there is a war, a riot, or a plague, it is always the working class who has to suffer the most, they have to suffer the loss of their loved ones, their own lives, their homes, and their freedom and dignity. Autarchs and the politicians were not severely hit by the wars as those people are just sitting in their luxurious palaces giving orders to wage wars and spread terror. Sadly, those orders to spread chaos and cause wars were followed by the members of the working class. Those soldiers went on to waste their lives on a fool's order. People like Shah Jahan loved to wage wars and spread terror, and they tried to justify it with religion. But those wars were not fought in the name of religion, those wars were fought in the name of hate, haughtiness, and undying greed asking for more and more. That greed cost the lives of thousands or even millions of soldiers and ordinary citizens belonging to the working class.

BENEVOLENT KING- People say that in the last years of his life, Shah Jahan became a benevolent and merciful king. It is incorrect as, during the last years of his life, he was no longer an emperor. He was sent to confinement, in simple words he was made a prisoner by his son Aurangzeb, Shah Jahan didn't have any power left as his son Aurangzeb became the mughal emperor. Without power and authority, he wasn't able to wage wars and oppress the innocents. He didn't become a benevolent and merciful king but he just became a powerless and authorityless prisoner during the last years of his life. He spent the last years of his life living in luxury while fulfilling all of his libidinous desires.

Moreover, even if we assume that he became a benevolent king during the last years of his reign due to the influence of his son, Dara Shukoh who held liberal views and was not a religious fanatic.[13,14,15] Still, it doesn't mean that he should be pardoned for all the nefarious crimes and heinous acts that he committed before becoming a benignant ruler. Pardoning him for all of his offences is the same as saying that the lives of thousands of hardworking ordinary citizens who were victims of these ferocious misdeeds and abuses do not matter, their lives were worthless and meaningless, they were born to die and suffer, that was their destiny. The life of a tyrannical despot like Shah Jahan matters as he was able to finally accept his savage malfeasances and crimes which he did on the hardworking civilians. He was finally able to have some guilt and remorse for the severe crimes he did just like his son Aurangzeb.[3] But if Shah Jahan really had remorse and guilt then why he didn't apologise to the citizens of his empire for the sufferings he had given them, why he hadn't documented that apology in his court chronicles? If he had apologised, then for sure the authors of his court chronicles could have mentioned that apology in every minute detail in a way to excessively glorify and magnify the emperor and also to please, flatter, and boast the king himself. He never publicly

Conclusion

apologised to the people for his crimes, neither any of his ancestors nor his descendants apologised for the monstrosities they had committed. Sadly, none of the tyrannical emperors like Shah Jahan were ever brought to justice for their crimes and wicked deeds. All of these despicable wretches spend their whole lives in luxury and comfort which were achieved at the expense of discomfort, abuse, and misery of the ordinary people of their empires. All of them lived long enough and they died only because of old age or natural causes.

Also, the Taj Mahal was not built by Shah Jahan out of love or affection towards his favourite wife Mumtaz Mahal which seems to me just a kind of show-off. If he built the Taj Mahal out of true love and undying affection, and in the memory of Mumtaz Mahal then why did he move to his new capital city Shahjahanabad (Old Delhi), why didn't he stayed at Agra where his true love was buried?[4] He could have kept Agra his capital city and nobody could have even dared to question his decision just like the rest of his decisions. Why the basic maintenance of the Taj Mahal was not done due to which the mausoleum started to enter a state of despair.[4] Why did he forget and neglect the Taj Mahal, why did he forget about the tomb of his wife, his true love, his children's mother as he didn't visit the Taj Mahal after 27th December, 1654?[5] Why does his son Aurangzeb have to write a letter to make him aware and remind him of the deteriorating condition of the Taj Mahal?[6]

The simple answer to these questions is that the Taj Mahal was not built by Shah Jahan out of love for his wife but it was built out of arrogance, ego, or maybe out of guilt if Shah Jahan had any as he was responsible for the death of his wife and also the lives of thousands of innocent souls. The names given or bestowed to these odious tyrants and sometimes these wretches named themselves would be enough to show their arrogant and egoistic nature.

For example, the name Shah Jahan translates to King of the World.[7] His father's name Jahangir translates to Conqueror of The World while the meaning of Akbar is greater (greatest).[8,9]

Alamgir which was another name for Aurangzeb translates to Conqueror of the World.[10] The other names by which Shah Jahan was referred were as follows Father of Victory, Star of the Faith, Warrior of Islam, Shah Jahan King of Kings, and so on.[11] In fact, this tyrant was so much drowned in his deep ocean of arrogance and pride that he started to view himself as somebody who comes next to god or the lord himself as his other names refer to him as Shadow of God on Earth, Muhammad the Second Lord of Conjunction.[11] The name and mighty titles which could have truly suited Shah Jahan, his character and his accomplishments should have been Thief of the World or King of Thieves, King of the Lust or King of the Horniness, Father of Hate, Star of the Fanatics, Shadow of Wickedness on Earth, Shah Jahan Saviour of Haters or Lover of Abusers, and many more like these. Shah Jahan built the Taj Mahal as an accomplishment, as a kind of statue or a some sort of remembrance. As there is a well-known saying that "The names of kings remain alive for ages on account of their buildings".[12] Jadunah Sarkar also claims that Shah Jahan wanted to be remembered. *(Jadunath Sarkar's words- This was an important job, as Shah Jahan was very fond of building noble edifices, – which will remain as his memorial to all time. (Sarkar, 1919, p. 10))*.[13] Shah Jahan just like every other king and emperor liked to be remembered after his death. He wanted future generations to remember him, his history, and the magnificent achievements that he had accomplished during his reign. Building the Taj Mahal was one of those splendid achievements and having his autobiographies officially written proves this claim of being remembered by future generations. He wanted the upcoming generations and the whole world to go through the history of India through his own eyes and perception. That's the reason why he erased and buried the history of millions of hardworking, warm-hearted citizens of India. All of those people become nameless and countless. Sadly, he succeeded in keeping himself immortal while creating and maintaining a positive image of being a true lover and a compassionate ruler. Our historians, our educational boards, our society, our politicians, our books, and media, you and I all are responsible for it as we helped this wicked monster in achieving his goals, ambitions, and desires. Because we gave importance to the life and achievements of a despotic tyrant instead of giving importance to the kind and naive civilians of that time. Our ancestors had to suffer at the hands of this barbaric autarch. Our ancestors were never able to taste the fruits of freedom, liberty, justice, equality, and secularism because of pathetic scumbags like Shah Jahan.

People like us love to visit the Taj Mahal. We love to give tiny replicas or models of the Taj Mahal as a gift to our loved ones, and to our partners. Our books love to share the epic 'love story' of a devilish tyrant and his true love. Our leaders, artists, public figures, and highly influential individuals in society love to visit the Taj Mahal just like everybody else. They love to take pictures over there. Maybe it was the President of the USA- a nation that is viewed as a beacon of freedom and equality, the President of France- a country which is considered as the birthplace of modern democracy along with the US or the Prime Minister of India- world's biggest democracy and home to hundreds of great individuals who fought for freedom and justice throughout their lives, and numerous public idols like these. All of these world figures love to take a picture in front of the Taj Mahal. A Shrine of Lies that was literally laid on the foundations of hate, oppression, inequality, barbaric pillaging, and religious bigotry. A shrine of lies that was built by a tyrant who committed various war crimes, genocides, and nefarious massacres of ordinary civilians.

Some individuals like me (when I was a kid) didn't know about the truth regarding Shah Jahan and the Taj Mahal while the others who knew it never tried to expose it to the world. None of those individuals exposed that lie, a lie that could have been exposed centuries ago but it wasn't. I believe that there might be some kind of a thought that could have been arising in your minds by now i.e. it is not the right time to unfold the truth as the people are not ready for it, as the world is not ready for it.

The simple answer is that society is never ready for a change, it is never ready for the truth when everybody has to spend their whole lives based on a lie. Truth is the only thing that can bring change. Change causes Revolution or Revolution causes Change.

If the people of France did not revolt against Louis XV1 because he was not ready for a change then we would never be able to see the French Revolution and if the French Revolution didn't happen then there would be no modern democracy. Democracy was the only thing that gave power to the common citizens, and it ended the monarchies and reigns of tyrannical despots from all across the world including India.

If the Allies could have waited to revolt against Hitler because he was not ready to end the holocaust. He could have never been stopped until he was able to execute every last standing Jew from the face of Earth. If the Guru Gobind Singh of Punjab or the Chhatrapati Shivaji Maharaj of the Maratha Empire did not revolted against the tyrant Aurangzeb because he was not ready for religious tolerance and liberty then his tyranny could have eaten all of India, its people, and its culture, its history, and its beauty. Due to their revolts and resistance, the era of these tyrannical dictators finally came to an end.

The Fugly Taj Mahal is not a monument of love, it was never a symbol of love. It can be a Symbol of Hate, a symbol of ruthless oppression, a symbol of tyranny, a symbol of uncounted war crimes, a symbol of lust, a symbol of lies, or a symbol of barbaric ransacking. It can be a symbol of any disgraceful, horrific, or immoral act but it can never be a symbol of love. It can be a monument of any kind of derogatory action but it could never be a monument of true love. It can be a temple of hate or a shrine of inhuman barbarities but it will never be a temple of undying love. It will always be a Shrine of Lies and always has been. The legacy of Shah Jahan is just like the legacy of the fugly Taj Mahal. He was not a true lover but a true hater. He was not a merciful or pitiful king but for sure he was a merciless and pitiless king. He was not a benevolent king, he was a tyrant, a barbarous despot. He was not a liberator, he was an oppressor. He was not the wealthiest emperor in the world, he was the richest thief in the world. He was the world's wealthiest plunderer, despot, and religious bigot but was never a true king. That's the hidden truth and now it has to be unfolded because everything that we knew, that we read, that we believe to be true regarding Shah Jahan and his Fugly Taj Mahal was a lie and always has been.

Chapter 12

Action

"That's one small step for a man, one giant leap for mankind."

-Neil Armstrong

Sadly, all the nameless innocent, benignant, hardworking civilians who had to endure torture, pain, oppression, who had to lose their lives and the lives of their loved ones, Innocents who had to lose their freedom, rights, and equality. We would never be able to give these souls a second chance, a chance to live freely, a chance to live with dignity and without fear and oppression, a chance to live with their loved ones in peace and harmony. All the intolerant disgusting tyrants like Shah Jahan who were responsible for the sufferings, abuse, and massacre of these poor considerate souls were able to get away with it. And we as human beings of the 21st century are still not smart enough or our technology is not that evolved or advanced that will help us to build a time machine. A time machine which will take us back to that era so that we could be able to save all those innocent lives and to bring all those monstrous autocrats to justice so to hang them all. I wished that we could do that but sadly, we can't. The only thing we can do, it's not the best but it's the 100% best we can give from our side.

Because it's not just about taking revenge but it's about sending a message. It's not just about vengeance but it's about teaching a lesson. A message loud enough that can be heard by everybody and that will reach every corner of the world, a lesson that's clear enough that can be taught to everybody, to every generation. That message, that lesson would be that true justice will be served at the end, it is inevitable, it could be delayed but it can never be prevented. Each and every last one of the wretches like the tyrant Shah Jahan will have to pay for the injustices which they did. These despicable wretches could have succeeded in delaying but they could have never been successful in averting the sword of true justice which kept on hanging around their necks like a predator in hiding waiting to strike on its prey at the right time. Justice will be served when the sword of true justice starts to strike through all the vile monuments and shrines of lies like the Taj Mahal, demolishing and burning these grotesque symbols of lies and atrocities down to the ground.

These shrines of lies were laid on the foundations of oppression, abuse, injustice, and discrimination of the weak, kind, virtuous, and hardworking civilians of the world. Shrines of Lies like the Taj Mahal were built by Shah Jahan out of arrogance and to show his magnificent achievements which in fact just consists of war crimes, massacres, and lust. These grotesque symbols of 'love' and 'peace' need to be burnt down to the ground and from the ashes of these shrines of lies, a better world will be built. Moreover, the Taj Mahal should be stripped of every honour, mention, and award that it has received throughout its meaningless existence. It should be stripped of the titles like being One of The Seven Wonders Of The World, UNESCO World Heritage Site and any other honours like these. Fugly Taj Mahal is not a symbol of love, it never was a symbol of love. The citizens of India, politicians, artists, world figures, and the entirety of human civilisation should boycott the Taj Mahal fully. They should stop visiting the Taj Mahal, they should stop buying and gifting merchandise related to the Taj Mahal. Worship of these shrines of lies should be stopped while idolisation of heartless monsters like Shah Jahan needs to be ended. Another point which also needs to be mentioned over here is that the whole empire of Shah Jahan was built on the foundations of barbaric plundering. So all these shining monuments and extravagant edifices like the Taj Mahal were also a byproduct of that ferocious marauding from the common hard working citizens of India who were our ancestors. This gives us the conclusion that everything from the white marble to the bricks which were used in the construction of Taj Mahal is rightfully ours as we are the descendants of those people from whom the wretched

Shah Jahan looted. We have the right to take these ransacked materials back to our homes because it's not just our right, it's our birthright. I am not trying to provoke anybody over here to do something violent or illegal, I am just trying to give one of the many reasons why Taj Mahal should be demolished. Also, I am not saying that we have to pick weapons or big hammers and start marching towards the Taj Mahal the next morning with a bulldozer.

The demolition of the Taj Mahal has to be done in a civilised, and legal way. Demolishing the Taj Mahal in a civilised way and under the jurisdiction of law is gonna differentiate us from tyrants like Shah Jahan. These wicked individuals ravaged lands and destroyed holy places in an uncivilised and unlawful way with the help of abuse of power, hate, and violence. On the other hand, we will never approach it this way, the demolition of the Taj Mahal will be achieved by peace and non-violence. In this way, we will prove that we are better than these pathetic wretches.

Note- The Author is not a lawyer and the author doesn't have any study related to law. In the next paragraphs, the author is just trying to give a basic idea and methods on how to sue and file a petition asking for the demolition of the Taj Mahal. For the best 100% accuracy and description on the procedure of filing a petition and winning the case, a lawyer consultation is a must.

The Taj Mahal is a property of India. The Supreme Court of India under the jurisdiction of the constitution of India has the right to take a decision regarding the future of the Taj Mahal. There is no doubt that the demolition of the Taj Mahal will receive criticism for sure. It will be affected by the dirty and corrupt politics of India as politicians will try to play the blame game. On top of that, some religious extremists will try to spread communal hate and religious propaganda regarding this matter. Along with that, the tourism industry will also play a major role in it. As per the official Taj Mahal website, around 7-8 million tourists visit the Taj Mahal annually.[1] If the Taj Mahal was demolished, the tourist industry around the Taj Mahal will suffer for sure. People will lose their jobs and businesses will shut down. There is a solution for this too and it will be discussed in the upcoming paragraphs.

First of all, Shah Jahan needs to be proven guilty for numerous war crimes, genocides, slavery, and crimes against humanity which he perpetrated on the populace of India. Secondly, he also needs to be proven guilty of taking away all the basic rights from the citizens of India. Third but not least, he also needs to be blamed and accused for playing and interfering with the evidence of his barbaric malefactions. Both the culprits and the victims are long gone (dead now) as it's nearly 400 years. So none of the culprits could be sued in court, especially the tyrant Shah Jahan but still, his marvellous monuments which are keeping him alive and immortal can be sued. The Court will only accept accusations which have evidence and proof, probably the written and officially documented records. The main evidence and proof that we have are those official court chronicles. The first two accusations will be easily proven with the help of his official court chronicles as those documents are written proof. Also, those were written under the jurisdiction of Shah Jahan so basically, he has already accepted that he committed these crimes. The third could also be proven with the help of those court chronicles as in those documents nothing is written regarding the living conditions of the working class during his reign. Also nothing has been mentioned regarding the aftermath of various war campaigns in which the imperial army went to ravaged lands and properties, and butchered innocents over there. Moreover, I am not able to find anything detailed regarding the living conditions of the working class during the reign of Shah Jahan even on the Internet. The books which I have read , there is little to none information regarding the life and living conditions of the working class. All of these books focus on the life and livelihood of the kings and the nobility. There is a little bit of mention of the working class in these books and I have to make my assumptions according to that information.

For sure, the famine that had happened in Gujarat and Deccan has been mentioned in his court chronicles but it has been only mentioned for the glorification of Shah Jahan and to portray him as a merciful, loving, and caring king. Whatever minor details that have been mentioned regarding the miserable and poor living conditions of the working class in V.A. Smith's books are primarily taken from the accounts of European travellers. There are just 2 main small detailed accounts (those small detailed accounts cover just 1-2 pages of the book) among which one deals with the living condition of the working class during the Gujarat-Deccan famine while the other deals with the ill-treatment and misery of the working class in the upper provinces of the Empire.[2,3] Jadunath Sarkar just mentions a couple of lines regarding the condition of the working class in his books.

Furthermore, it is also to be noted that Jadunath Sarkar's views on Shah Jahan are neutral as he hadn't mentioned a lot of details and personal opinions regarding the character of Shah Jahan as compared to V.A. Smith. On the other hand, V.A. Smith has heavily criticised Shah Jahan due to which many other historians have called V.A. Smith's opinions on Shah Jahan as totally biased.[4] This creates a possibility that the opinions and incidents mentioned by V.A. Smith in his book could not be considered worthy enough for evidence against Shah Jahan's offences. Also, some authors believe that the writings of European travellers are not authentic and it is also considered biased.[5] Even Jadunath Sarkar criticises the work of European writers in his book Studies in Mughal India (Sarkar, 1919).[6] B.P. Saksena also criticises the overall work of European travellers but still, he also believes that some records mentioned by European travellers like Bernier and Mundy are true and unbiased (Saksena, 1932).[7] One point needs to be mentioned over here which is that both Jadunath Sarkar and B.P. Saksena wrote these books when India was still a colony of the British Empire and during that time, a lot of nationalist movements were ongoing in India asking for Independence from the British Empire. As both Jadunath Sarkar and B.P. Saksena were Indians, and their criticism and disapproval of European travellers could have been influenced by these nationalist movements. On the contrary, K.S. Lal considers the writings of the European travellers to be objective and factual; he also states that *"European travellers did not 'invent' scandals; they wrote only what 'they heard or what they saw."* (Lal, 1988, p. 6).[8]

Personally, I totally disagree with the historians who consider V.A. Smith or European travellers as biased. The main reason behind it is that all the other writers, histories, and books have portrayed Shah Jahan as a loving, caring, and merciful Emperor. Even though he carried out the same atrocious deeds just like his son Aurangzeb who has been viewed as a ruthless and cruel potentate. Shah Jahan was just like him as he committed crimes of fratricides and he brought back the policies of religious intolerance and many other barbaric enormities were done by him. V.A. Smith is the only writer who tries to shed light on the brutish character and dark past of Shah Jahan which had been either denied, buried, or totally overlooked by other historians. That's the reason why he has been criticised and declared as biased by other historians because he didn't follow the same trend of glorification and idealisation of Shah Jahan as a benevolent and loving king like the majority of historiographers who followed it. Fergus Nicoll also criticises Shah Jahan but not that much as compared to V.A. Smith.

It looks like Shah Jahan didn't want us to know about his heinous crimes and that's the reason why the available informative material regarding the work-life and living conditions of the ordinary people during his reign is little to nothing. The only accessible details are taken from the writings of foreign travellers who were not Indian citizens and on whose writings Shah Jahan didn't have any jurisdiction or control. That's why the history of millions of innocents had been entirely wiped out in a bid to protect and save the history of one single individual, not even a single individual but a heartless tyrant.

Other crimes of Shah Jahan like the oppression and abuse of women in his harem, the abuse of workers of the Taj Mahal, or the maternal death of Mumtaz Mahal would be harder to prove. Historians like K.S. Lal and V.A. Smith mentions the overall abuse of women in the harem as a whole in the mughal reign (I mean during the entire era of the mughal dynasty in India). They didn't mention Shah Jahan and the abuse of women in his harem specifically. It is basically because there is a lack of evidence and secondly, also some of these assumptions are viewed as a myth. Even though some of these are viewed as a myth, still there could be a 50-50% possibility of these myths being true or false. Frankly speaking, we don't even need to prove these myths are true as court chronicles gave enough evidence that will help us to win the case with ease and without any difficulty. But still, if we think about the worst-case scenario, the Supreme Court denies the petition to demolish the Taj Mahal and the case has been closed.

Then in that situation, we can still win. If you ask how are we gonna win after the Supreme Court has denied to give permission to demolish the Taj Mahal? It's pretty simple and easy. There is one simple word which is *Unity*. With unity, we can easily make the Supreme Court reconsider its decision. If every Indian and every citizen of the world unite against the Taj Mahal, then no power on Earth would be able to prevent Shah Jahan and his shrine of lies from meeting its fate. By unifying, I don't mean that we have to join a mob that will march towards the Taj Mahal, protest against it and go to demolish and burn it down to the ground by itself. We don't have to protest, the protests, blockage of roads, and railway routes are only gonna make the working class suffer and it is gonna affect their day-to-day activities. We don't want it to happen and we should prevent it from happening at any cost. We have to bring Shah Jahan to justice with the help of non-violence and in a civilised way. With Unity, all of us should boycott the grotesque Taj Mahal.

We should stop visiting the Taj Mahal and stop buying stuff and accessories which resemble or link to the Taj Mahal or Shah Jahan. We have to boycott businesses and places that survive on that shrine of lies. People who work at the Taj Mahal site should quit their jobs right away. Not only boycott but we also have to spread awareness and truth regarding the atrocities of Shah Jahan and his shrine of lies. Not only India but the whole world should become aware of it and it can be easily achieved with the help of the internet and social media these days. We can start several hashtag trends like #BoycottTajMahal, #CancelTajMahal, #DemolishTajMahal on most popular global social media sites like Twitter, Instagram, Facebook etc. and with these trends we could be able to make this issue a hot topic on social media around the world. Idolization and worshipping of these shrines of lies needs to be stopped. Moreover, the government officials, politicians of India, artists, actors, prominent individuals and world figures also need to boycott this monument. If the Tourist Industry got hit brutally as nobody is visiting or working at the Taj Mahal and also, the image of India started to deteriorate around the entire world because people got to know about the atrocious past of the Shah Jahan and the fugly Taj Mahal. Then maybe, under these situations, the Supreme Court would be automatically pressured to reconsider its decision of not allowing the demolition of the Taj Mahal. I don't think that we will ever be in this kind of situation. But, still if we got into it then the only way to win it over would be unity among us all.

Furthermore, I am not saying that after the demolition of the Taj Mahal we have to leave that area unattended and nothing else has to be built over there. If that place is kept unattended, it's probably gonna turn into some kind of a junkyard. As I have said earlier, the tourism industry whose income totally relies on the Taj Mahal will be severely hit as those people will entirely lose their source of income and living. Mainly due to the sudden decline in the number of tourists visiting the Taj Mahal. Tourists will stop going to visit the demolished area of the Taj Mahal as there is nothing else watchable left over there. The working class again has to suffer as the people will lose their jobs and businesses in that area. We don't want it to happen because we are not like the pitiless Shah Jahan whose ego and arrogance had made countless innocent and hard toiling citizens suffer. This situation can easily be prevented with a simple solution and that solution will also make our case against the demolition of the Taj Mahal even stronger.

That simple solution is that something has to be built instead of the grotesque Taj Mahal over there. In that area, we can plant trees or build a greenhouse to fight against climate change and also to control the pollution levels. A beautiful garden can also be built as it will help us to save bees and many more things like that which will help us in saving our planet and making it look more beautiful. In my opinion, the best thing that we can build over there instead of the lust mahal is a museum. A Museum that will work as a Shrine of Truth instead of a Shrine of Lies. A magnificent museum that is dedicated to honouring and remembering all those ordinary hard-working citizens of India who were victims of oppression and hate during the reign of abusers like Shah Jahan. A museum devoted to all the women and girls who were victims of sexual abuse and discrimination during the times of war or invasion by foreign swines. A museum dedicated to the 20000 nameless daily wage workers and labourers who had to build a shrine of lies to fulfil the arrogant and egoist demands and needs of a tyrant. A museum which will help us to remember various revolts and revolutions led by brave freedom fighters and world figures who stood and fought for the justice, rights, and liberties which we enjoy today. A museum that holds statues of real heroes and freedom fighters of India like Guru Gobind Singh, Chhatrapati Shivaji Maharaj, Shaheed Bhagat Singh, Shaheed Udham Singh and many more. A museum which isn't only built to honour and remember the Indian freedom fighters but also to the world figures who also had made countless sacrifices and saved human society from evil. World freedom fighters and world figures like Abraham Lincoln of the US, Nelson Mandela of South Africa, Mother Teresa, and many more individuals like them should also be honoured by erecting their statues in the museum. Guru Nanak Dev Ji told us the difference between goodness and wickedness. Guru

Nanak Dev also stood for women's empowerment and rights, Jesus Christ who sacrificed himself for our sins, Gautama Buddha who told us not to lie and accept the truth, and several other religious and spiritual saints like these can also be honoured in that museum.[9] Moreover, the museum shouldn't only contain their statues and images but it should also contain their ideology and core beliefs. These things will help us to truly understand the meaning of freedom, justice, peace, and harmony. These things will also help us to understand the difference between good and evil, right and wrong.

There is also another way if the Government of India or Supreme Court still didn't allow the demolition of the Taj Mahal and also if the Taj Mahal hasn't been stripped of any honours, titles, or awards bestowed on it. Then in that case scenario, it's not the best but the least good we can do. It is that the people, society, influential figures, and politicians shouldn't visit the Taj Mahal by keeping in mind it as a symbol of love instead they should view it and keep in mind that they are visiting a symbol of hate and oppression. They are visiting a shrine of lies laid on the foundations of war crimes, pillaging, and abuse of the weak and the poor.

Also, the media, the whole internet, and websites dedicated to the Taj Mahal should portray the Taj Mahal as a symbol of hate and abuse. By just changing the word love to hate in the definition of Taj Mahal in every corner of the world, we will also be able to honour all those soft-hearted, hard working civilians who had to suffer and lose their lives at the hands of wretched tyrants like Shah Jahan.

Visiting and worshipping a monument laid on the foundations of hate and oppression, idolizing and glamorizing a scoundrel individual, an animal, or a tyrant responsible for the manslaughter and genocide of countless innocent civilians needs to be stopped and that shrine of lies has to be burnt down. There is still evil present and its presence can be felt in every corner of the world. Fierce tyrants like Shah Jahan who were the core followers of that devilry and hate left something behind to remind us of them and their disgusting achievements. Just like the Taj Mahal, other monuments like Red Fort and Agra Fort were also built by this wretch. Even tombs of despotic autocrats like Aurangzeb are also present and preserved which don't deserve to be preserved and adored. We used to have a road known as the Aurangzeb road in Delhi which was renamed afterward to Dr. APJ Abdul Kalam road in 2015.[10] If the name of a road can be changed then monuments and shrines of lies like the ugly Taj Mahal can also be demolished. Just like these monuments, there could have been 100s or even 1000s of these shrines of lies which can be found all over the world. I don't know about the history of all the nations, communities, and cultures but natives of those nations and cultures knew better if they also have monuments and shrines of lies like the fugly Taj Mahal which shouldn't be standing and being worshipped as those monuments were also built by tyrants. Then those monuments also need to face the same fate as the wretched Taj Mahal.

The decision regarding the demolition of the Taj Mahal entirely depends on the Supreme Court of India but the fate of the Taj Mahal depends on us. By us, I mean the working class, virtuous, and kind people who built this world. Whoever is still reading it, I am talking to you right now and before you make any decision, just sit down if you are standing. Sat down in a quiet place free of noise and any disturbances. Read the upcoming text first and then close your eyes. Now put yourself into the shoes of a daily wage worker, a peasant, a farmer, or any common citizen of the working class who is alive during the reign of Shah Jahan. I mean just take yourself back in time.

Let's begin with your birth. Luckily, you were born in a family that follows the same religion as the state religion of Shah Jahan. So Shah Jahan who is conservative and also religious intolerant to different religions other than his own is not gonna come for you or your family to hurt you or to force you to change your religion. But still, there could be a possibility that you have to serve in the imperial army whose only objective is to demolish and mutilate places belonging to other religions, ravage lands, and massacre warm-hearted citizens of independent states. The imperial army does not have any set of morals or a code of conduct due to which it just keeps on viciously butchering people and annihilating lands. You also have to do the same, you have to kill innocents and destroy property because that's the order that you receive and that's what every other soldier in the imperial army is doing. You don't want to do it but you have to, if you fail to do it then your loyalty to your commander and the tyrant Shah Jahan would be questioned and you can put your life and your family's life in grave danger as you are given the title of a traitor.

Unluckily, you were born into a family that doesn't follow the state religion. In this scenario your life would have been worse, it would have become hell during that time. You and your family always had to live under the fear of losing their freedom, home, your loved ones, neighbours or relatives if your nation was ever attacked by the heartless tyrant. You always had to be ready for the war and the women in your household always had to be ready to hide. Your mother, your daughter, your wife, your sister, or any other woman in your household is not safe from the perverted eyes of the imperial army and the tyrant himself. If you or your family do not accept the state religion then everybody in your household will lose their lives and their honour.

The worst of all, the unluckiest among these is being born as a woman during those times. Being dead was better than being born as a woman during those times. You don't have any rights or freedom, you don't have a right because you are not a living creature. You are a property of the men, you are just a thing, a child-bearing machine or a pleasuring toy and that's all. If you belong to the enemy state and it gets attacked, then it doesn't matter if you accept their state religion or not as at the end of the day you will be treated as a trophy. If the army commanders or the emperor don't find you charming enough to live in the harem, then you would be given to the perverted imperial army. No matter where they sent you, the wretches over there will eat up your dignity, self-respect, and self-worth like f**king hyenas. Your beauty is not gonna be a blessing but it's gonna be a curse for you. You can't use the word No as that word shouldn't exist in your vocabulary, your No doesn't matter, the word No doesn't suit your tongue. You are a loyal servant to the men and saying No to your masters shows your disloyalty and disrespect towards them.

The word Yes will prove your obedience and respect towards Shah Jahan or his men. You have to say Yes to whatever the men, your masters tell you to do. You have to spend your entire life fulfilling their demands, their happiness, and their wishes. Their desires and their demands are yours. You don't have your own demands and wishes, even though if you have some wishes that don't matter, those desires are always gonna come in last place after their own wishes (by last, I mean the very last, even after the needs of their dogs and pets). That's how you are gonna spend the rest of your life which is not even yours, it's theirs. That's all I have to say and now you can open your eyes and you are free to come out of your imagination to the present day. Now you are free to make a decision, a choice that is gonna be yours because you have the right and freedom to make that selection. The rights and freedoms that those tender-hearted considerate people never had. I have already made my decision.

If you wonder how I have made my decision, it's pretty simple. I will tell you the trick that helped me to make my choice. I am not sure if my decision will only be accepted by me or if it will be converted from me to we. Before making the decision, I looked at my surroundings and people, I looked at the face of my mother who raised me, my father who paid for my education, my grandfather who was a farmer, my sister and my female classmates who were studying diligently to achieve their dreams, my female co-workers, strangers sitting in the bus going to work, or to do groceries, or to meet their loved ones or to go back home after a tiring day; cops who were trying to keep us safe and many more individuals like them. There is one common thing among all and it is that all of them are law-abiding citizens who are trying to create a better life for themselves and their loved ones, and a better world for all. Then I wonder if these kind individuals were born during the reign of wretches like Shah Jahan, would they have gotten respect, justice, equality, peace, and a better life. Then I made my choice. My decision was not to just stop at the demolition of the Taj Mahal, it begins from there.

If you still believe that Shah Jahan does not deserve this fate and the Taj Mahal does not need to be demolished; you still support and favours Shah Jahan over the innocent, hard-working , kind-hearted souls; you still believe that Shah Jahan needs to be pardoned for his crimes, we have to show mercy and politeness to him. In this scenario, I would like to ask you something. Do you think Shah Jahan would have shown you mercy, kindness if you had questioned him, revolted against him or said No to his state religion or to his sexual favours? Would Shah Jahan have fought for your dignity and self-respect? Would Shah Jahan have provided care and protection for you and your family from the morally decayed imperial army which was ravaging your independent state? There are many such questions that can be presented. Think about it and then consider your decision. But still if your decision or views regarding Shah Jahan haven't changed a single bit even after considering these scenarios and you still want to justify Shah Jahan and fight for him, then I would like to tell you (My personal opinion, it can be wrong) that you are just as morally decayed like the tyrant Shah Jahan. You should go for rehabilitation as soon as possible as you are forgetting or already lost the basic social principles, humanism, etiquettes, and moral values. If the purge ever happens in the distinct future and the mob of criminals, rioters, murderers, or terrorists is running on the streets whose only mission and main purpose is to destroy peace with chaos, mow down justice with injustice, and burn down every last thing that represents a civilised and lawful world; I wouldn't be surprised if I found you leading, or following that mob. Sorry if you feel attacked or hurt but that's the truth, a possibility or a reality.

But on the other hand, I will fight for every nameless, innocent soul that has to endure pain and sufferings at the hands of brutal tyrants like Shah Jahan. Ordinary people like us have to lose their rights and freedom. People like us lost their lives and the lives of their loved ones. Women like our mothers, daughters and sisters have to lose their dignity and self-respect. I will give them justice just like we fight for our justice. I will fight for their honour just like we will fight for our dignity. I will fight for their freedoms just like we fight for our liberties and rights. I will boycott all those ugly monuments and shrines of lies like the fugly Taj Mahal which were laid on the foundations of oppression of soft-hearted courteous citizens like us. I will expunge the history and meaningless accomplishments of uncultured swines like Shah Jahan. Their history and gruesome accomplishments will be wiped out in the same way as they erased the history and life of millions of kind-hearted hardworking civilians. I spit on their monuments and their graves. I will never honour these ungrateful bastards and their worthless, meaningless lives. The life of a single kind-hearted hardworking soul is worth a million times more than all the combined lives of every tyrant and worthless criminal to ever exist on the face of Earth. I will learn from the inhuman brutalities that mankind did in the past and that it is still doing in the present.

By not repeating those mistakes, a better, and more prosperous future and world will be created. By fighting for those nameless and unknown souls, we are fighting for ourselves, we are fighting for our own freedom and rights. By admiring those innocent souls, we are honouring ourselves. By revering and cherishing those nameless molested women, we are honouring our partners, mothers, sisters, and daughters. Because we and those people are mirrored images of each other.

It is because of us and them that this world is still out here, it is because of us and them that there is still kindness in this world, it is because of their sacrifices and sufferings that we are able to enjoy the liberties and rights which they never had. Eventually, they will receive the acclamation which they deserve, and tyrants like Shah Jahan and their shrine of lies will be brought to justice. These contemptible wretches and their shrines of lies will pay for it, I will fight until my last breath for that justice and freedom.

If you join me, a revolution will be born and also if you oppose me, a revolution will be delayed. A Revolution can never be stopped, it can only be delayed. It can be delayed for days, months, years, or even centuries but one day it will be out there. A revolution is the only thing that will help us to build a better world- a better world which is not just about us or them, but for everybody and for the greater good of all mankind. With justice, equality, and revolutions, a better world will be built that will eventually lay the foundations for Elysium.

MAKE THIS WORLD A BETTER PLACE
#FOR ALL

Thank You
IZ

Bibliography

Note- The readers will find page numbers mentioned at the end of every book reference (in some cases even online articles too). This has been done to make it easier for individuals who want to read, double check or compare the information and facts provided by the author with the original source. The author would still recommend going through the whole source material mainly because some cases create a possibility of written information or some lines being influenced by the entire book(s) or article(s).

Chapter 1- INTRODUCTION

1. Google. (n.d.). Shrine. *In Google Dictionary (Provided by Oxford Languages)*. Retrieved November 21, 2022, from https://www.google.com/search?q=google+dictionary&rlz=1CAEVJI_enCA903CA903&oq=google+dic&aqs=chrome.2.69i57j0i512l2j0i10i131i433i512j0i512l4j0i10i131i433i512l2.4021j0j15&sourceid=chrome&ie=UTF-8#dobs=shrine

2. Google. (n.d.). Temple. *In Google Dictionary (Provided by Oxford Languages)*. Retrieved November 22, 2022, from https://www.google.com/search?q=temple+definition&rlz=1CAEVJI_enCA903CA903&oq=temple+def&aqs=chrome.0.69i59j69i57j0i512l8.4398j0j15&sourceid=chrome&ie=UTF-8

3. Koshal. (2011, May 28). *Difference between temple and shrine.* Difference Between. https://www.differencebetween.com/difference-between-temple-and-vs-shrine/

4. Google. (n.d.). Monument. *In Google Dictionary (Provided by Oxford Languages)*. Retrieved November 22, 2022, from https://www.google.com/search?q=monument+definition&rlz=1CAEVJI_enCA903CA903&sxsrf=ALiCzsYxtpuqrvUu8h-fu5J7F14r8cpUNQ%3A1669084029812&ei=fTN8Y_GRMfCxptQP5vyHuAQ&oq=monument+def&gs_lcp=Cgxnd3Mtd2l6LXNlcnAQARgAMgkIIxAnEEYQ-QEyBQgAEIAEMgUIABCABDIFCAAQgAQyBQgAEIAEMgUIABCABDIFCAAQgAQyBQgAEIAEMgUIABCABDIFCAA

Bibliography

QhgM6BwgjEOoCECc6BwguEOoCECc6BAgjECc6BAgAEEM
6CgguEMcBEK8BEEM6BwgAELEDEEM6CggAELEDEIMBEE
M6EQguEK8BEMcBEJIDEMkDEIAEOhEILhCABBCxAxDHA
RCvARDUAjoICC4QgAQQ1AI6CwgAEIAEELEDEIMBOggI
ABCxAxCRAjoLCC4Q1AIQsQMQgAQ6DgguELEDEIMBEMc
BEK8BOgUILhCABDoICAAQgAQQsQM6CwguEIAEEMcBE
K8BOgsILhCvARDHARCABEoECEEYAEoECEYYAFCiA1id
GWDvJGgBcAF4AIABlQKIAZQQkgEGMC4xMS4xmAEAoA
EBsAEKwAEB&sclient=gws-wiz-serp

5. Google. (n.d.). World Heritage Site. *In Google Dictionary (Provided by Oxford Languages)*. Retrieved November 22, 2022, from https://www.google.com/search?q=world+heritage+sites+definition&rlz=1CAEVJI_enCA903CA903&sxsrf=ALiCzsZglmPuzvNZSiMAnKggA7hkZNIFMA%3A1669087582319&ei=XkF8Y76FE5WeptQPnoOV6AU&oq=world+heritage+site&gs_lcp=Cgxnd3Mtd2l6LXNlcnAQARgAMgcIIxCwAxAnMgoIABBHENYEELADMgoIABBHENYEELADMgoIABBHENYEELADMgoIABBHENYEELADMgoIABBHENYEELADMgoIABBHENYEELADMgoIABBHENYEELADMgoIABBHENYEELADMgcIABCwAxBDMgcIABCwAxBDMgcIABCwAxBDMg0IABDkAhDWBBCwAxgBMg0IABDkAhDWBBCwAxgBMg0IABDkAhDWBBCwAxgBMhUILhDHARCvARDUAhDIAxCwAxBDGAIyEgguEMcBEK8BEMgDELADEEMYAjIVCC4QxwEQrwEQ1AIQyAMQsAMQQxgCMhIILhDHARCvARDIAxCwAxBDGAJKBAhBGABKBAhGGAFQAFgAYP8MaAFwAXgAgAEAiAEAkgEAmAEAyAETwAEB2gEGCAEQARgJ2gEGCAIQARgI&sclient=gws-wiz-serp

6. National Park Service. (2022, October 7). *Statue of Liberty*. https://www.nps.gov/stli/index.htm

7. Gujarat Tourism. (n.d.). *Statue of Unity*. https://www.gujarattourism.com/central-zone/narmada/statue-of-unity.html

8. History.com Editors. (2009, November 9). *Bombing of Hiroshima and Nagasaki*. HISTORY. https://www.history.com/topics/world-war-ii/bombing-of-hiroshima-and-nagasaki

9. UNESCO World Heritage Convention. (n.d.). *Hiroshima peace memorial (Genbaku Dome)*. https://whc.unesco.org/en/list/775

10. New 7 Wonders Foundation. (n.d.). *New 7 wonders of the world.* https://world.new7wonders.com/

11. New 7 Wonders Foundation. (n.d.). *New 7 wonders of the world.* https://world.new7wonders.com/

12. UNESCO World Heritage Convention. (n.d.). *Taj Mahal.* https://whc.unesco.org/en/list/252/

13. Taj Mahal Official Website. (n.d.). *Emperor Shah Jahan :: Maker of The Taj Mahal.* tajmahal.gov.in. https://www.tajmahal.gov.in/maker-of-the-taj-mahal.aspx

14. Nicoll, F. (2009). *Shah Jahan: The rise and fall of the mughal emperor.* Haus Publishing Ltd. Page 243

15. UNESCO World Heritage Convention. (n.d.). *Taj Mahal.* https://whc.unesco.org/en/list/252/

16. Times of India Author. (2007, July 6). Last minute rush to vote for Taj in the seven wonders poll. *The Times of India.* https://timesofindia.indiatimes.com/india/last-minute-rush-to-vote-for-taj-in-the-seven-wonders-poll/articleshow/2182738.cms

17. Taj Mahal Official Website. (n.d.). *Emperor Shah Jahan:: About Shah Jahan.* Tajmahal.gov.in. https://www.tajmahal.gov.in/about-shah-Jahan.aspx

Chapter 2- LOVE OR LUST

1. Official Taj Mahal Website. (n.d.). *Emperor Shah Jahan :: Maker of the Taj Mahal.* Tajmahal.gov.in. https://www.tajmahal.gov.in/maker-of-the-taj-mahal.aspx

2. Nicoll, F. (2009). *Shah Jahan: The rise and fall of the mughal emperor.* Haus Publishing Ltd. Page- 95 and 167

3. Saksena, B. P. (1932). *History of Shah Jahan of Dilhi.* The Indian Press.

OR

Bibliography

Saksena, B. P. (1932). *History of Shah Jahan of Dilhi.* Internet Archive (Provided by Digital Library of India aka Public Library of India). https://archive.org/details/in.ernet.dli.2015.281500/mode/1 up?view=theater Page 11

4. Official Taj Mahal Website. (n.d.). *Emperor Shah Jahan :: Maker of the Taj Mahal.* Tajmahal.gov.in. https://www.tajmahal.gov.in/about-shah-Jahan.aspx

5. Official Taj Mahal Website. (n.d.). *The cause of the taj:: Mumtaz Mahal:: Mumtaz Mahal.* Tajmahal.gov.in. https://www.tajmahal.gov.in/the-cause-of-the-taj.aspx

6. Official Taj Mahal Website. (n.d.). *The cause of the taj:: Mumtaz Mahal:: Mumtaz Mahal.* Tajmahal.gov.in. https://www.tajmahal.gov.in/the-cause-of-the-taj.aspx

7. Official Taj Mahal Website. (n.d.). *The cause of the taj:: Mumtaz Mahal:: Mumtaz Mahal.* Tajmahal.gov.in. https://www.tajmahal.gov.in/the-cause-of-the-taj.aspx

8. Official Taj Mahal Website. (n.d.). *Empress Mumtaz Mahal.* Tajmahal.gov.in. https://www.tajmahal.gov.in/about-mumtaz-mahal.aspx

9. Nicoll, F. (2009). *Shah Jahan: The rise and fall of the mughal emperor.* Haus Publishing Ltd. Page- 176

10. Nicoll, F. (2009). *Shah Jahan: The rise and fall of the mughal emperor.* Haus Publishing Ltd. Page- 174 and 176

11. March of Dimes Organisation. (2021, May). *Maternal death and pregnancy-related death.* https://www.marchofdimes.org/find-support/topics/miscarriage-loss-grief/maternal-death-and-pregnancy-related-death

12. March of Dimes Organisation. (May, 2017). *Neonatal death.* https://www.marchofdimes.org/find-support/topics/miscarriage-loss-grief/neonatal-death

13. March of Dimes Organisation. (October, 2020). *Stillbirth.* *https://www.marchofdimes.org/find-support/topics/miscarriage-loss-grief/stillbirth*

14. Tidy, Dr Colin. (2019, Jan 21). *Gravidity and parity definitions.* Patient. https://patient.info/doctor/gravidity-and-parity-definitions-and-their-implications-in-risk-assessment#:~:text=Gravidity%20is%20defined%20as%20the,born%20alive%20or%20was%20stillborn

15. Murray, D. (2022, June 24). *Maternal mortality rate, causes, and prevention.* Very Well Family. https://www.verywellfamily.com/maternal-mortality-rate-causes-and-prevention-4163653#citation-6

16. NDTV Author. (2017, July 11). World population day: How many children can a woman safely deliver? *NDTV.* https://www.ndtv.com/health/world-population-day-how-many-children-can-a-woman-safely-deliver-1723242

17. NDTV Author. (2017, July 11). World population day: How many children can a woman safely deliver? *NDTV.* https://www.ndtv.com/health/world-population-day-how-many-children-can-a-woman-safely-deliver-1723242

18. NDTV Author. (2017, July 11). World population day: How many children can a woman safely deliver? *NDTV.* https://www.ndtv.com/health/world-population-day-how-many-children-can-a-woman-safely-deliver-1723242

19. March of Dimes Organisation. (2020, March). *Postpartum hemorrhage.* https://www.marchofdimes.org/find-support/topics/postpartum/postpartum-hemorrhage#:~:text=Postpartum%20hemorrhage%20(also%20called%20PPH)%20is%20when%20a%20woman%20has,to%205%20percent)%20have%20PPH.

20. March of Dimes Organisation. (2017, July). *How long should you wait before getting pregnant again?* https://www.marchofdimes.org/find-support/topics/planning-baby/how-long-should-you-wait-getting-pregnant-again

21. Bellefonds, Colleen de. (2022, April 26). *How soon after giving birth can you get pregnant?* What to Expect. https://www.whattoexpect.com/pregnancy/pregnancy-health/how-soon-can-you-get-pregnant-after-giving-birth/

Bibliography

22. Kumar, A. (2014). *Monument of love or symbol of maternal death: The story behind the Taj Mahal*. Research Gate. https://www.researchgate.net/publication/263967169_Monument_of_Love_or_Symbol_of_Maternal_Death_The_Story_Behind_the_Taj_Mahal

    DOI- https://doi.org/10.1016/j.crwh.2014.07.001

23. Nicoll, F. (2009). *Shah Jahan: The rise and fall of the mughal emperor*. Haus Publishing Ltd. Page- 256-260

24. Kumar, A. (2014). *Monument of love or symbol of maternal death: The story behind the Taj Mahal*. Research Gate. https://www.researchgate.net/publication/263967169_Monument_of_Love_or_Symbol_of_Maternal_Death_The_Story_Behind_the_Taj_Mahal

    DOI- https://doi.org/10.1016/j.crwh.2014.07.001

25. Nicoll, F. (2009). *Shah Jahan: The rise and fall of the mughal emperor*. Haus Publishing Ltd. Page- 171

26. Nicoll, F. (2009). *Shah Jahan: The rise and fall of the mughal emperor*. Haus Publishing Ltd. Page- 171

27. Lal, K. S. (1988). *The mughal harem*. Aditya Prakashan. Page- 83

28. Lal, K. S. (1988). *The mughal harem*. Aditya Prakashan. Page- 157

29. Marhol, Dr Andrei. (2021, February 4). *Ancient birth control methods: How did women prevent pregnancy throughout the ages?* Flo Health. https://flo.health/menstrual-cycle/sex/birth-control/ancient-birth-control-methods

30. History of birth control. (2022, October 3). In *Wikipedia*. https://en.wikipedia.org/w/index.php?title=History_of_birth_control&oldid=1113751316

31. Lal, K. S. (1988). *The mughal harem*. Aditya Prakashan. Page- 146

32. Marhol, Dr Andrei. (2021, February 4). *Ancient birth control methods: How did women prevent pregnancy throughout the ages?*

Flo Health. https://flo.health/menstrual-cycle/sex/birth-control/ancient-birth-control-methods

33. Srivastava, A. L. (1986). *The mughul empire* (8th ed.). Shiva Lal Agarwala & Company. Page- 299 First edition published- 1952

Chapter 3- HAREM

1. Google. (n.d.). Harem. *In Google Dictionary (Provided by Oxford Languages)*. Retrieved December 11, 2022, from https://www.google.com/search?q=harem+definition&rlz=1 CAEVJI_enCA903CA903&oq=harem+definition&aqs=chrome.. 69i57j0i512l9.3800j1j15&sourceid=chrome&ie=UTF-8

2. Current Publishing Author. (2017, May 8). *Column: Agra fort and its harem*. You Are Current. https://www.youarecurrent.com/2017/05/08/column-agra-fort-and-its-harem/#:~:text=Estimates%20of%20the%20number%20of,and%20dance%20for%20his%20pleasure

AND

Safvi, R. (2016, December 21). *We now know what went inside the mughal harems*. Dailyo. https://www.dailyo.in/variety/mughal-royal-harem-voyeurism-erotic-instincts-shah-jahan-14650

3. News Crab Author. (n.d.). *Shah Jahan was the most lustful emperor in mughal history! Had a relationship with daughter, after the death of his wife*. Dailyhunt. https://m.dailyhunt.in/news/india/english/newscrab-epaper-dh32db7fdb07694f23a2e9e08cf334911b/shah+jahan+was+the+most+lustful+emperor+in+mughal+history+had+a+relationsh ip+with+daughter+after+the+death+of+his+wife-newsid-n186287316

4. Anjum, F. (2011, June). *Strangers' gaze: Mughal harem and european travellers of the seventeenth century*. Research Gate. https://www.researchgate.net/publication/317012204_Strangers%27_Gaze_Mughal_Harem_and_European_Travellers_of_the_Seventeenth_Century Page- 72

Bibliography

5. Lal, K. S. (1988). *The mughal harem*. Aditya Prakashan. Page- 37 and 72

6. Lal, K. S. (1988). *The mughal harem*. Aditya Prakashan. Page- 37 and 38

7. Niccolao Manucci. (2022, November 17). In *Wikipedia*. https://en.wikipedia.org/wiki/Niccolao_Manucci

8. Anjum, F. (2011, June). *Strangers' gaze: Mughal harem and european travellers of the seventeenth century*. Research Gate. https://www.researchgate.net/publication/317012204_Strangers%27_Gaze_Mughal_Harem_and_European_Travellers_of_the_Seventeenth_Century Page- 72

9. Lal, K. S. (1988). *The mughal harem*. Aditya Prakashan. Page- 19, 20 and 25

10. Lal, K. S. (1988). *The mughal harem*. Aditya Prakashan.Page- 165 and 166

11. Anjum, F. (2011, June). *Strangers' gaze: Mughal harem and european travellers of the seventeenth century*. Research Gate. https://www.researchgate.net/publication/317012204_Strangers%27_Gaze_Mughal_Harem_and_European_Travellers_of_the_Seventeenth_Century Page- 75

12. Google. (n.d.). Eunuch. In *Google Dictionary (Provided by Oxford Languages)*. Retrieved December 11, 2022, from https://www.google.com/search?q=eunuch+definition&rlz=1CAEVJI_enCA903CA903&oq=eunuch+de&aqs=chrome.0.0i512j69i57j0i512l8.3993j1j15&sourceid=chrome&ie=UTF-8

13. Lal, K. S. (1988). *The mughal harem*. Aditya Prakashan. Page- 165 and 187

14. Anjum, F. (2011, June). *Strangers' gaze: Mughal harem and european travellers of the seventeenth century*. Research Gate. https://www.researchgate.net/publication/317012204_Strangers%27_Gaze_Mughal_Harem_and_European_Travellers_of_the_Seventeenth_Century Page- 75

15. Lal, K. S. (1988). *The mughal harem*. Aditya Prakashan.Page- 11

16. Elliot, H. M. (1875). *Shah Jahan*. Internet Archive (Provided by Cornell University Library and Digitilised by Microsoft Corporation). https://archive.org/details/cu31924006140374/Page/n5/mode/2up Page- 36 and 45

17. Lal, K. S. (1988). *The mughal harem*. Aditya Prakashan. Page- 165

18. Sal's Thoughts. (2021, November 12). *The sex lives of women inside a mughal emperor's harem*. Medium. https://medium.com/lessons-from-history/the-sex-lives-of-women-inside-a-mughal-emperors-harem-10124c18260b

    OR

    Lal, K. S. (1988). *The mughal harem*. Aditya Prakashan.

19. Lal, K. S. (1988). *The mughal harem*. Aditya Prakashan. Page- 30

20. Lal, K. S. (1988). *The mughal harem*. Aditya Prakashan. Page- 30 and 31

21. Sal's Thoughts. (2021, November 12). *The sex lives of women inside a mughal emperor's harem*. Medium. https://medium.com/lessons-from-history/the-sex-lives-of-women-inside-a-mughal-emperors-harem-10124c18260b

22. Lal, K. S. (1988). *The mughal harem*. Aditya Prakashan.

23. Lal, K. S. (1988). *The mughal harem*. Aditya Prakashan.Page- 53

24. Safvi, R. (2016, December 21). *We now know what went inside the mughal harems*. Dailyo. https://www.dailyo.in/variety/mughal-royal-harem-voyeurism-erotic-instincts-shah-jahan-14650

25. Historia Maxima- History Stories. (2020, June 8). *What life was really like inside a medieval mughal harem in India* [Video]. YouTube. https://www.youtube.com/watch?v=gfVub-rFTwI

26. Lal, K. S. (1988). *The mughal harem*. Aditya Prakashan. Page- 120 and 179

Bibliography

27. Nicoll, F. (2009). *Shah Jahan: The rise and fall of the mughal emperor.* Haus Publishing Ltd. Page- 73

28. Lal, K. S. (1988). *The mughal harem.* Aditya Prakashan. Page- 114, 115 and 131

29. Lal, K. S. (1988). *The mughal harem.* Aditya Prakashan. Page- 44 and 61

30. Lal, K. S. (1988). *The mughal harem.* Aditya Prakashan. Page- 179 and 180

31. Sal's Thoughts. (2021, November 12). *The sex lives of women inside a mughal emperor's harem.* Medium. https://medium.com/lessons-from-history/the-sex-lives-of-women-inside-a-mughal-emperors-harem-10124c18260b

32. Lal, K. S. (1988). *The mughal harem.* Aditya Prakashan. Page- 179 and 180

33. Safvi, R. (2016, December 21). *We now know what went inside the mughal harems.* Dailyo. https://www.dailyo.in/variety/mughal-royal-harem-voyeurism-erotic-instincts-shah-jahan-14650

34. Lal, K. S. (1988). *The mughal harem.* Aditya Prakashan.

35. Sal's Thoughts. (2021, November 12). *The sex lives of women inside a mughal emperor's harem.* Medium. https://medium.com/lessons-from-history/the-sex-lives-of-women-inside-a-mughal-emperors-harem-10124c18260b

36. Lal, K. S. (1988). *The mughal harem.* Aditya Prakashan. Page- 181 and 187

37. Lal, K. S. (1988). *The mughal harem.* Aditya Prakashan. Page- 38, 51 and 52

38. Anjum, F. (2011, June). *Strangers' gaze: Mughal harem and european travellers of the seventeenth century.* Research Gate. https://www.researchgate.net/publication/317012204_Strangers%27_Gaze_Mughal_Harem_and_European_Travellers_of_the_Seventeenth_Century Page- 73

39. Lal, K. S. (1988). *The mughal harem*. Aditya Prakashan. Page- 53 and 187

40. Sal's Thoughts. (2021, November 12). *The sex lives of women inside a mughal emperor's harem*. Medium. https://medium.com/lessons-from-history/the-sex-lives-of-women-inside-a-mughal-emperors-harem-10124c18260b

41. Historia Maxima- History Stories. (2020, June 8). *What life was really like inside a medieval mughal harem in India* [Video]. YouTube. https://www.youtube.com/watch?v=gfVub-rFTwI

42. Lal, K. S. (1988). *The mughal harem*. Aditya Prakashan. Page- 56, 104 and 144

43. Lal, K. S. (1988). *The mughal harem*. Aditya Prakashan. Page- 30 and 44

44. Sal's Thoughts. (2021, November 12). *The sex lives of women inside a mughal emperor's harem*. Medium. https://medium.com/lessons-from-history/the-sex-lives-of-women-inside-a-mughal-emperors-harem-10124c18260b

45. Lal, K. S. (1988). *The mughal harem*. Aditya Prakashan. Page- 152

46. Anjum, F. (2011, June). *Strangers' gaze: Mughal harem and european travellers of the seventeenth century*. Research Gate. https://www.researchgate.net/publication/317012204_Strangers%27_Gaze_Mughal_Harem_and_European_Travellers_of_the_Seventeenth_Century Page- 72 and 73

47. Safvi, R. (2016, December 21). *We now know what went inside the mughal harems*. Dailyo. https://www.dailyo.in/variety/mughal-royal-harem-voyeurism-erotic-instincts-shah-jahan-14650

48. Lal, K. S. (1988). *The mughal harem*. Aditya Prakashan. Page- 92 and 163

49. Francois Bernier. (2022, December 3). In *Wikipedia*. https://en.wikipedia.org/wiki/Fran%C3%A7ois_Bernier

Bibliography

50. Saksena, B. P. (1932). *History of Shah Jahan of Dilhi*. Internet Archive (Provided by Digital Library of India aka Public Library of India). https://archive.org/details/in.ernet.dli.2015.281500/mode/1up?view=theaterPage- 336 to 338

51. Peter Mundy. (2022, May 15). In *Wikipedia*. https://en.wikipedia.org/wiki/Peter_Mundy

52. Lal, K. S. (1988). *The mughal harem*. Aditya Prakashan.Page- 92,93 and 163

53. Saksena, B. P. (1932). *History of Shah Jahan of Dilhi*. Internet Archive (Provided by Digital Library of India aka Public Library of India). https://archive.org/details/in.ernet.dli.2015.281500/mode/1up?view=theater Page- 336 to 340

54. Lal, K. S. (1988). *The mughal harem*. Aditya Prakashan. Page- 168

55. Saksena, B. P. (1932). *History of Shah Jahan of Dilhi*. Internet Archive (Provided by Digital Library of India aka Public Library of India). https://archive.org/details/in.ernet.dli.2015.281500/mode/1up?view=theaterPage- x x iii

56. Johan Albrecht de Mandelslo. (2019, June 22). In *Wikipedia*. https://en.wikipedia.org/wiki/Johan_Albrecht_de_Mandelslo

57. Lal, K. S. (1988). *The mughal harem*. Aditya Prakashan. Page- 193

58. Lal, K. S. (1988). *The mughal harem*. Aditya Prakashan. Page- 163

59. Lal, K. S. (1988). *The mughal harem*. Aditya Prakashan. Page- 148

60. Smith, V. A. (1919). *The oxford history of India: From the earliest times to the end of 1911*. Internet Archive (Provided by University of Toronto).

https://archive.org/details/oxfordhistoryofi00smituoft/Page/321/mode/1up Page- 415

61. Lal, K. S. (1988). *The mughal harem.* Aditya Prakashan. Page- 204

62. Saksena, B. P. (1932). *History of Shah Jahan of Dilhi.* Internet Archive (Provided by Digital Library of India aka Public Library of India). https://archive.org/details/in.ernet.dli.2015.281500/mode/1up?view=theater Page- 336

63. Lal, K. S. (1988). *The mughal harem.* Aditya Prakashan. Page- 204

64. Lal, K. S. (1988). *The mughal harem.* Aditya Prakashan. Page- 205

65. Srivastava, A. L. (1986). *The mughul empire* (8th ed.). Shiva Lal Agarwala & Company. Page- 298 First edition published- 1952

66. K. S. Lal. (2022, February 2). In *Wikipedia.* https://en.wikipedia.org/wiki/K._S._Lal

Chapter 4- COURT CHRONICLES

1. Vedantu Author. (n.d.). *Questions & answers- What do you mean by court chronicles?* Vedantu. https://www.vedantu.com/question-answer/what-do-you-mean-by-court-chronicles-class-7-social-science-cbse-60b8d7e2af283c55ef8e93b1

2. Elliot, H. M. (1875). *Shah Jahan.* Internet Archive (Provided by Cornell University Library and Digitilised by Microsoft Corporation). https://archive.org/details/cu31924006140374/Page/n5/mode/2up Page- 3

OR

Elliot, H. M. (1875). *Shah Jahan.* Hafiz Press Lahore.

3. Elliot, H. M. (1875). *Shah Jahan.* Internet Archive (Provided by Cornell University Library and Digitilised by Microsoft

Bibliography

Corporation). https://archive.org/details/cu31924006140374/Page/n5/mode/2upPage- 80

4. Elliot, H. M. (1875). *Shah Jahan*. Internet Archive (Provided by Cornell University Library and Digitilised by Microsoft Corporation). https://archive.org/details/cu31924006140374/Page/n5/mode/2up

5. Henry Miers Elliot. (2022, August 4). In *Wikipedia*. https://en.wikipedia.org/wiki/Henry_Miers_Elliot

6. Elliot, H. M. (1875). *Shah Jahan*. Internet Archive (Provided by Cornell University Library and Digitilised by Microsoft Corporation). https://archive.org/details/cu31924006140374/Page/n5/mode/2upPage- 4

7. Elliot, H. M. (1875). *Shah Jahan*. Internet Archive (Provided by Cornell University Library and Digitilised by Microsoft Corporation). https://archive.org/details/cu31924006140374/Page/n5/mode/2upPage- 81

8. Elliot, H. M. (1875). *Shah Jahan*. Internet Archive (Provided by Cornell University Library and Digitilised by Microsoft Corporation). https://archive.org/details/cu31924006140374/Page/n5/mode/2upPage- 4

9. Saksena, B. P. (1932). *History of Shah Jahan of Dilhi*. Internet Archive (Provided by Digital Library of India aka Public Library of India). https://archive.org/details/in.ernet.dli.2015.281500/mode/1up?view=theaterPage- 336

10. Elliot, H. M. (1875). *Shah Jahan*. Internet Archive (Provided by Cornell University Library and Digitilised by Microsoft Corporation). https://archive.org/details/cu31924006140374/Page/n5/mode/2upPage- 6

11. Elliot, H. M. (1875). *Shah Jahan.* Internet Archive (Provided by Cornell University Library and Digitilised by Microsoft Corporation).
https://archive.org/details/cu31924006140374/Page/n5/mode/2upPage- 6,7

12. Elliot, H. M. (1875). *Shah Jahan.* Internet Archive (Provided by Cornell University Library and Digitilised by Microsoft Corporation).
https://archive.org/details/cu31924006140374/Page/n5/mode/2up

13. Elliot, H. M. (1875). *Shah Jahan.* Internet Archive (Provided by Cornell University Library and Digitilised by Microsoft Corporation).
https://archive.org/details/cu31924006140374/Page/n5/mode/2up

14. Elliot, H. M. (1875). *Shah Jahan.* Internet Archive (Provided by Cornell University Library and Digitilised by Microsoft Corporation).
https://archive.org/details/cu31924006140374/Page/n5/mode/2up

15. Elliot, H. M. (1875). *Shah Jahan.* Internet Archive (Provided by Cornell University Library and Digitilised by Microsoft Corporation).
https://archive.org/details/cu31924006140374/Page/n5/mode/2upPage- 129

16. Elliot, H. M. (1875). *Shah Jahan.* Internet Archive (Provided by Cornell University Library and Digitilised by Microsoft Corporation).
https://archive.org/details/cu31924006140374/Page/n5/mode/2up

17. Elliot, H. M. (1875). *Shah Jahan.* Internet Archive (Provided by Cornell University Library and Digitilised by Microsoft Corporation).
https://archive.org/details/cu31924006140374/Page/n5/mode/2up

Bibliography

18. Elliot, H. M. (1875). *Shah Jahan*. Internet Archive (Provided by Cornell University Library and Digitilised by Microsoft Corporation). https://archive.org/details/cu31924006140374/Page/n5/mode/2upPage- 26 and 27

19. Smith, V. A. (1919). *The oxford history of India: From the earliest times to the end of 1911*. Internet Archive (Provided by University of Toronto). https://archive.org/details/oxfordhistoryofi00smituoft/Page/321/mode/1upPage- 393 and 394

20. Elliot, H. M. (1877). *The history of India as told by its own historians: The muhammadan period* (Vol. 7) (J. Dowson, Ed.). Internet Archive (Provided by Digital Library of India aka Public Library of India). https://archive.org/details/in.ernet.dli.2015.501804/Page/n5/mode/2upPage- 35

Chapter 5- OTHER CRIMES AND ATROCITIES OF SHAH JAHAN

Book- HISTORY OF AURANGZIB, VOLUME 1- REIGN OF SHAH JAHAN

1. Jadunath Sarkar. (2022, October 30). In *Wikipedia*. https://en.wikipedia.org/wiki/Jadunath_Sarkar

2. BYJU'S Author. (n.d.). *Question-answer: Persian was the official language of the Mughals*. BYJU'S. https://byjus.com/question-answer/was-the-official-language-of-the-mughals-hindipersiansanskrittamil-2/

OR

Lal, K. S. (1988). *The mughal harem*. Aditya Prakashan.Page- 1

3. Sarkar, J. (1912). *History of aurangzib: Mainly based on persian sources* (Vol. 1: Reign of Shah Jahan). Internet Archive (Provided by Digital Library of India aka Public Library of India and National Archives of India). https://archive.org/details/dli.granth.88707/mode/1up Page- 27

OR

Sarkar, J. (1912). *History of aurangzib: Mainly based on persian sources* (Vol. 1: Reign of Shah Jahan). M.C. Sarkar & Sons.

4. Sarkar, J. (1912). *History of aurangzib: Mainly based on persian sources* (Vol. 1: Reign of Shah Jahan). Internet Archive (Provided by Digital Library of India aka Public Library of India and National Archives of India). https://archive.org/details/dli.granth.88707/mode/1up Page- 29

5. Sarkar, J. (1912). *History of aurangzib: Mainly based on persian sources* (Vol. 1: Reign of Shah Jahan). Internet Archive (Provided by Digital Library of India aka Public Library of India and National Archives of India). https://archive.org/details/dli.granth.88707/mode/1up Page- 37

6. Elliot, H. M. (1875). *Shah Jahan.* Internet Archive (Provided by Cornell University Library and Digitilised by Microsoft Corporation). https://archive.org/details/cu31924006140374/mode/1up?view=theater Page- 59

7. Sarkar, J. (1912). *History of aurangzib: Mainly based on persian sources* (Vol. 1: Reign of Shah Jahan). Internet Archive (Provided by Digital Library of India aka Public Library of India and National Archives of India). https://archive.org/details/dli.granth.88707/mode/1up Page- 55

8. Sarkar, J. (1912). *History of aurangzib: Mainly based on persian sources* (Vol. 1: Reign of Shah Jahan). Internet Archive (Provided by Digital Library of India aka Public Library of India and National Archives of India). https://archive.org/details/dli.granth.88707/mode/1up Page- 62 and 63

9. Sarkar, J. (1912). *History of aurangzib: Mainly based on persian sources* (Vol. 1: Reign of Shah Jahan). Internet Archive (Provided by Digital Library of India aka Public Library of India and National Archives of India).

https://archive.org/details/dli.granth.88707/mode/1up
Page- 171

10. Sarkar, J. (1912). *History of aurangzib: Mainly based on persian sources* (Vol. 1: Reign of Shah Jahan). Internet Archive (Provided by Digital Library of India aka Public Library of India and National Archives of India). https://archive.org/details/dli.granth.88707/mode/1up
Page- 176 and 177

11. Nicoll, F. (2009). *Shah Jahan: The rise and fall of the mughal emperor*. Haus Publishing Ltd. Page- 199

12. Sarkar, J. (1912). *History of aurangzib: Mainly based on persian sources* (Vol. 1: Reign of Shah Jahan). Internet Archive (Provided by Digital Library of India aka Public Library of India and National Archives of India). https://archive.org/details/dli.granth.88707/mode/1up
Page- 180

13. Smith, V. A. (1919). *The oxford history of India: From the earliest times to the end of 1911*. Internet Archive (Provided by University of Toronto). https://archive.org/details/oxfordhistoryofi00smituoft/Page/321/mode/1up

14. Sarkar, J. (1912). *History of aurangzib: Mainly based on persian sources* (Vol. 1: Reign of Shah Jahan). Internet Archive (Provided by Digital Library of India aka Public Library of India and National Archives of India). https://archive.org/details/dli.granth.88707/mode/1up
Page- 249

15. Sarkar, J. (1912). *History of aurangzib: Mainly based on persian sources* (Vol. 1: Reign of Shah Jahan). Internet Archive (Provided by Digital Library of India aka Public Library of India and National Archives of India). https://archive.org/details/dli.granth.88707/mode/1up
Page- 269 and 274

16. Sarkar, J. (1912). *History of aurangzib: Mainly based on persian sources* (Vol. 1: Reign of Shah Jahan). Internet Archive (Provided by Digital Library of India aka Public Library of

India and National Archives of India).
https://archive.org/details/dli.granth.88707/mode/1up
Page- 276

17. Elliot, H. M. (1875). *Shah Jahan*. Internet Archive (Provided by Cornell University Library and Digitilised by Microsoft Corporation).
https://archive.org/details/cu31924006140374/Page/n5/mode/2up

18. Sarkar, J. (1912). *History of aurangzib: Mainly based on persian sources* (Vol. 1: Reign of Shah Jahan). Internet Archive (Provided by Digital Library of India aka Public Library of India and National Archives of India).
https://archive.org/details/dli.granth.88707/mode/1up
Page-283

19. Srivastava, A. L. (1986). *The mughul empire* (8th ed.). Shiva Lal Agarwala & Company. Page- 298 First edition published- 1952

Book- HISTORY OF AURANGZIB, VOLUME 2- WAR OF SUCCESSION

1. Sarkar, J. (1912). *History of aurangzib: Mainly based on persian sources* (Vol. 2: War of Succession). Internet Archive (Provided by Digital Library of India aka Public Library of India). https://archive.org/details/in.ernet.dli.2015.23814/Page/n2/mode/1up?view=theater Page- 78

OR

Sarkar, J. (1912). *History of aurangzib: Mainly based on persian sources* (Vol. 2: War of Succession). M.C. Sarkar & Sons.

2. Sarkar, J. (1912). *History of aurangzib: Mainly based on persian sources* (Vol. 2: War of Succession). Internet Archive (Provided by Digital Library of India aka Public Library of India). https://archive.org/details/in.ernet.dli.2015.23814/Page/n2/mode/1up?view=theater Page- 84

Bibliography

Book- THE OXFORD HISTORY OF INDIA

1. Murphy, D. (2009, October). *Smith, Vincent Arthur*. Dictionary of Irish Biography. https://www.dib.ie/biography/smith-vincent-arthur-a8154

2. Thomas Roe. (2022, October 1). In *Wikipedia*. https://en.wikipedia.org/wiki/Thomas_Roe

3. Smith, V. A. (1919). *The oxford history of India: From the earliest times to the end of 1911*. Internet Archive (Provided by University of Toronto). https://archive.org/details/oxfordhistoryofi00smituoft/Page/321/mode/1up Page- 383

OR

Smith, V. A. (1919). *The oxford history of India: From the earliest times to the end of 1911*. Clarendon Press.

4. Smith, V. A. (1919). *The oxford history of India: From the earliest times to the end of 1911*. Internet Archive (Provided by University of Toronto). https://archive.org/details/oxfordhistoryofi00smituoft/Page/321/mode/1up Page- 384

5. Smith, V. A. (1919). *The oxford history of India: From the earliest times to the end of 1911*. Internet Archive (Provided by University of Toronto). https://archive.org/details/oxfordhistoryofi00smituoft/Page/321/mode/1up Page- 393

6. Elliot, H. M. (1875). *Shah Jahan*. Internet Archive (Provided by Cornell University Library and Digitilised by Microsoft Corporation). https://archive.org/details/cu31924006140374/Page/n5/mode/2up

7. Elliot, H. M. (1875). *Shah Jahan*. Internet Archive (Provided by Cornell University Library and Digitilised by Microsoft Corporation). https://archive.org/details/cu31924006140374/Page/n5/mode/2up Page- 26 and 27

8. Nicoll, F. (2009). *Shah Jahan: The rise and fall of the mughal emperor.* Haus Publishing Ltd. Page- 198

9. Elliot, H. M. (1875). *Shah Jahan.* Internet Archive (Provided by Cornell University Library and Digitilised by Microsoft Corporation). https://archive.org/details/cu31924006140374/Page/n5/mode/2up Page- 48 and 49

10. Swamy, K. R. N. (2003, April 13). Treasures the mughals emperors owned. *Tribune India.* https://www.tribuneindia.com/2003/20030413/spectrum/heritage.htm

11. Purnima, P. (n.d.). *Revenue administration under the mughals.* History Discussion. https://www.historydiscussion.net/history-of-india/mughal-empire/revenue-administration-under-the-mughals/6235

12. Sarkar, J. (1919). *Studies in mughal India.* Internet Archive (Provided by University of Toronto). https://archive.org/details/studiesinmughali00sarkuoft/mode/1up Page- 16

13. Nicoll, F. (2009). *Shah Jahan: The rise and fall of the mughal emperor.* Haus Publishing Ltd. Page- 299

14. Elliot, H. M. (1875). *Shah Jahan.* Internet Archive (Provided by Cornell University Library and Digitilised by Microsoft Corporation). https://archive.org/details/cu31924006140374/Page/n5/mode/2up Page- 147

15. Official Taj Mahal Website. (n.d.). *Emperor Shah Jahan :: Maker of The Taj Mahal.* Tajmahal.gov.in. https://www.tajmahal.gov.in/maker-of-the-taj-mahal.aspx

16. Nicoll, F. (2009). *Shah Jahan: The rise and fall of the mughal emperor.* Haus Publishing Ltd. Page- 198

17. Smith, V. A. (1919). *The oxford history of India: From the earliest times to the end of 1911.* Internet Archive (Provided by University of Toronto).

Bibliography

https://archive.org/details/oxfordhistoryofi00smituoft/Page/321/mode/1up Page- 393 and 394

18. Smith, V. A. (1919). *The oxford history of India: From the earliest times to the end of 1911*. Internet Archive (Provided by University of Toronto). https://archive.org/details/oxfordhistoryofi00smituoft/Page/321/mode/1up Page- 399

19. Smith, V. A. (1919). *The oxford history of India: From the earliest times to the end of 1911*. Internet Archive (Provided by University of Toronto). https://archive.org/details/oxfordhistoryofi00smituoft/Page/321/mode/1up Page- 403

20. Elliot, H. M. (1875). *Shah Jahan*. Internet Archive (Provided by Cornell University Library and Digitilised by Microsoft Corporation). https://archive.org/details/cu31924006140374/Page/n5/mode/2up Page- 111

21. Smith, V. A. (1919). *The oxford history of India: From the earliest times to the end of 1911*. Internet Archive (Provided by University of Toronto). https://archive.org/details/oxfordhistoryofi00smituoft/Page/321/mode/1up Page- 404

22. Smith, V. A. (1919). *The oxford history of India: From the earliest times to the end of 1911*. Internet Archive (Provided by University of Toronto). https://archive.org/details/oxfordhistoryofi00smituoft/Page/321/mode/1up Page- 407

23. Smith, V. A. (1919). *The oxford history of India: From the earliest times to the end of 1911*. Internet Archive (Provided by University of Toronto). https://archive.org/details/oxfordhistoryofi00smituoft/Page/321/mode/1up Page- 415

24. Smith, V. A. (1919). *The oxford history of India: From the earliest times to the end of 1911*. Internet Archive (Provided by University of Toronto).

https://archive.org/details/oxfordhistoryofi00smituoft/Page/321/mode/1up Page- 416

25. Sarkar, J. (1912). *History of aurangzib: Mainly based on persian sources* (Vol. 1: Reign of Shah Jahan). Internet Archive (Provided by Digital Library of India aka Public Library of India and National Archives of India). https://archive.org/details/dli.granth.88707/mode/1up Page - 180

26. Smith, V. A. (1919). *The oxford history of India: From the earliest times to the end of 1911.* Internet Archive (Provided by University of Toronto). https://archive.org/details/oxfordhistoryofi00smituoft/Page/321/mode/1up Page- 416 and 417

27. Smith, V. A. (1919). *The oxford history of India: From the earliest times to the end of 1911.* Internet Archive (Provided by University of Toronto). https://archive.org/details/oxfordhistoryofi00smituoft/Page/321/mode/1up Page- 418

28. Smith, V. A. (1919). *The oxford history of India: From the earliest times to the end of 1911.* Internet Archive (Provided by University of Toronto). https://archive.org/details/oxfordhistoryofi00smituoft/Page/321/mode/1up Page- 419

29. Smith, V. A. (1919). *The oxford history of India: From the earliest times to the end of 1911.* Internet Archive (Provided by University of Toronto). https://archive.org/details/oxfordhistoryofi00smituoft/Page/321/mode/1up Page- 421

30. Saksena, B. P. (1932). *History of Shah Jahan of Dilhi.* Internet Archive (Provided by Digital Library of India aka Public Library of India). https://archive.org/details/in.ernet.dli.2015.281500/mode/1up?view=theater Page- 293 and 294

31. Smith, V. A. (1919). *The oxford history of India: From the earliest times to the end of 1911.* Internet Archive (Provided by University of Toronto).

Bibliography

https://archive.org/details/oxfordhistoryofi00smituoft/Page/321/mode/1up Page- 466

32. Smith, V. A. (1919). *The oxford history of India: From the earliest times to the end of 1911*. Internet Archive (Provided by University of Toronto). https://archive.org/details/oxfordhistoryofi00smituoft/Page/321/mode/1up Page- 415

33. Smith, V. A. (1919). *The oxford history of India: From the earliest times to the end of 1911*. Internet Archive (Provided by University of Toronto). https://archive.org/details/oxfordhistoryofi00smituoft/Page/321/mode/1up Page- 465

Book- THE OXFORD STUDENT'S HISTORY OF INDIA

1. Smith, V. A. (1921). *The oxford student's history of India* (9th ed.). Internet Archive (Provided by University of Toronto). https://archive.org/details/oxfordstudentshi00smituoft/Page/151/mode/1up?view=theater Page- 199

OR

Smith, V. A. (1921). *The oxford student's history of India* (9th ed.). Clarendon Press.

2. Smith, V. A. (1921). *The oxford student's history of India* (9th ed.). Internet Archive (Provided by University of Toronto). https://archive.org/details/oxfordstudentshi00smituoft/Page/151/mode/1up?view=theater Page- 200

AND

Jean-Baptiste Tavernier. (2022, December 5). In *Wikipedia*. https://en.wikipedia.org/wiki/Jean-Baptiste_Tavernier

3. Smith, V. A. (1921). *The oxford student's history of India* (9th ed.). Internet Archive (Provided by University of Toronto). https://archive.org/details/oxfordstudentshi00smituoft/Page/151/mode/1up?view=theater Page- 203

4. Smith, V. A. (1921). *The oxford student's history of India* (9th ed.). Internet Archive (Provided by University of Toronto).

https://archive.org/details/oxfordstudentshi00smituoft/Page/151/mode/1up?view=theater Page- 204

5. Smith, V. A. (1921). *The oxford student's history of India* (9th ed.). Internet Archive (Provided by University of Toronto). https://archive.org/details/oxfordstudentshi00smituoft/Page/151/mode/1up?view=theater Page- 221

6. Smith, V. A. (1921). *The oxford student's history of India* (9th ed.). Internet Archive (Provided by University of Toronto). https://archive.org/details/oxfordstudentshi00smituoft/Page/151/mode/1up?view=theater Page- 184

Book- SHAH JAHAN: THE RISE AND FALL OF THE MUGHAL EMPEROR

1. Nicoll, F. (2009). *Shah Jahan: The rise and fall of the mughal emperor.* Haus Publishing Ltd. Page- ix

2. Nicoll, F. (2009). *Shah Jahan: The rise and fall of the mughal emperor.* Haus Publishing Ltd. Page- 74

3. Nicoll, F. (2009). *Shah Jahan: The rise and fall of the mughal emperor.* Haus Publishing Ltd. Page- 89

4. Nicoll, F. (2009). *Shah Jahan: The rise and fall of the mughal emperor.* Haus Publishing Ltd. Page- 127

5. Nicoll, F. (2009). *Shah Jahan: The rise and fall of the mughal emperor.* Haus Publishing Ltd. Page- 199

6. Nicoll, F. (2009). *Shah Jahan: The rise and fall of the mughal emperor.* Haus Publishing Ltd. Page- 199

7. Nicoll, F. (2009). *Shah Jahan: The rise and fall of the mughal emperor.* Haus Publishing Ltd. Page- 20

8. Nicoll, F. (2009). *Shah Jahan: The rise and fall of the mughal emperor.* Haus Publishing Ltd. Page- 198 to 200

9. Nicoll, F. (2009). *Shah Jahan: The rise and fall of the mughal emperor.* Haus Publishing Ltd. Page- 247

Bibliography

Book- THE SHAH JAHAN HANDBOOK: EVERYTHING YOU NEED TO KNOW ABOUT SHAH JAHAN

Note- This book is accessed online via the kobo website. The Page numbers mentioned here can vary depending on the factors such as font size, screen size, type of device etc. which the reader is using while accessing this book online.

1. Mcgee, R. (2016). *The Shah Jahan handbook- Everything you need to know about Shah Jahan.* Emereo Publishing. https://www.kobo.com/ca/en/ebook/the-shah-jahan-handbook-everything-you-need-to-know-about-shah-jahan Page- 36 of 52, Introduction

2. Nicoll, F. (2009). *Shah Jahan: The rise and fall of the mughal emperor.* Haus Publishing Ltd. Page- 87

3. Mcgee, R. (2016). *The Shah Jahan handbook- Everything you need to know about Shah Jahan.* Emereo Publishing. https://www.kobo.com/ca/en/ebook/the-shah-jahan-handbook-everything-you-need-to-know-about-shah-jahan Page- 6 of 60, Shah Jahan 3

4. Nicoll, F. (2009). *Shah Jahan: The rise and fall of the mughal emperor.* Haus Publishing Ltd. Page- 199

5. Mcgee, R. (2016). *The Shah Jahan handbook- Everything you need to know about Shah Jahan.* Emereo Publishing. https://www.kobo.com/ca/en/ebook/the-shah-jahan-handbook-everything-you-need-to-know-about-shah-jahan Page- 25 of 60

6. Mcgee, R. (2016). *The Shah Jahan handbook- Everything you need to know about Shah Jahan.* Emereo Publishing. https://www.kobo.com/ca/en/ebook/the-shah-jahan-handbook-everything-you-need-to-know-about-shah-jahan Page- 30 of 60

Book- HISTORY OF SHAHJAHAN OF DILHI

1. Banarsi Prasad Saksena. (2020, March 30). In *Wikipedia.* https://en.wikipedia.org/wiki/Banarsi_Prasad_Saxena

2. Saksena, B. P. (1932). *History of Shah Jahan of Dilhi*. Internet Archive (Provided by Digital Library of India aka Public Library of India). https://archive.org/details/in.ernet.dli.2015.281500/mode/1up?view=theater Page- x x iii

3. Saksena, B. P. (1932). *History of Shah Jahan of Dilhi*. Internet Archive (Provided by Digital Library of India aka Public Library of India). https://archive.org/details/in.ernet.dli.2015.281500/mode/1up?view=theater Page- 29

4. Saksena, B. P. (1932). *History of Shah Jahan of Dilhi*. Internet Archive (Provided by Digital Library of India aka Public Library of India). https://archive.org/details/in.ernet.dli.2015.281500/mode/1up?view=theater Page- 46

5. Saksena, B. P. (1932). *History of Shah Jahan of Dilhi*. Internet Archive (Provided by Digital Library of India aka Public Library of India). https://archive.org/details/in.ernet.dli.2015.281500/mode/1up?view=theater Page- 81 and 82

6. Saksena, B. P. (1932). *History of Shah Jahan of Dilhi*. Internet Archive (Provided by Digital Library of India aka Public Library of India). https://archive.org/details/in.ernet.dli.2015.281500/mode/1up?view=theater Page- 85

7. Saksena, B. P. (1932). *History of Shah Jahan of Dilhi*. Internet Archive (Provided by Digital Library of India aka Public Library of India). https://archive.org/details/in.ernet.dli.2015.281500/mode/1up?view=theater

Page- 89 and 90

8. Saksena, B. P. (1932). *History of Shah Jahan of Dilhi*. Internet Archive (Provided by Digital Library of India aka Public Library of India). https://archive.org/details/in.ernet.dli.2015.281500/mode/1up?view=theater Page- 117

9. Saksena, B. P. (1932). *History of Shah Jahan of Dilhi.* Internet Archive (Provided by Digital Library of India aka Public Library of India). https://archive.org/details/in.ernet.dli.2015.281500/mode/1up?view=theater Page- 118

10. Saksena, B. P. (1932). *History of Shah Jahan of Dilhi.* Internet Archive (Provided by Digital Library of India aka Public Library of India). https://archive.org/details/in.ernet.dli.2015.281500/mode/1up?view=theater Page- 136

11. Saksena, B. P. (1932). *History of Shah Jahan of Dilhi.* Internet Archive (Provided by Digital Library of India aka Public Library of India). https://archive.org/details/in.ernet.dli.2015.281500/mode/1up?view=theater Page- 156

12. Elliot, H. M. (1875). *Shah Jahan.* Internet Archive (Provided by Cornell University Library and Digitilised by Microsoft Corporation). https://archive.org/details/cu31924006140374/Page/n5/mode/2up

13. Sarkar, J. (1912). *History of aurangzib: Mainly based on persian sources* (Vol. 1: Reign of Shah Jahan). Internet Archive (Provided by Digital Library of India aka Public Library of India and National Archives of India). https://archive.org/details/dli.granth.88707/mode/1up

14. Saksena, B. P. (1932). *History of Shah Jahan of Dilhi.* Internet Archive (Provided by Digital Library of India aka Public Library of India). https://archive.org/details/in.ernet.dli.2015.281500/mode/1up?view=theater Page- 158 and 159

15. Saksena, B. P. (1932). *History of Shah Jahan of Dilhi.* Internet Archive (Provided by Digital Library of India aka Public Library of India). https://archive.org/details/in.ernet.dli.2015.281500/mode/1up?view=theater Page- 174

16. Saksena, B. P. (1932). *History of Shah Jahan of Dilhi*. Internet Archive (Provided by Digital Library of India aka Public Library of India). https://archive.org/details/in.ernet.dli.2015.281500/mode/1up?view=theater Page- 192

17. Saksena, B. P. (1932). *History of Shah Jahan of Dilhi*. Internet Archive (Provided by Digital Library of India aka Public Library of India). https://archive.org/details/in.ernet.dli.2015.281500/mode/1up?view=theater Page- 227

18. Saksena, B. P. (1932). *History of Shah Jahan of Dilhi*. Internet Archive (Provided by Digital Library of India aka Public Library of India). https://archive.org/details/in.ernet.dli.2015.281500/mode/1up?view=theater Page- 234

19. Saksena, B. P. (1932). *History of Shah Jahan of Dilhi*. Internet Archive (Provided by Digital Library of India aka Public Library of India). https://archive.org/details/in.ernet.dli.2015.281500/mode/1up?view=theater Page- 292

20. Saksena, B. P. (1932). *History of Shah Jahan of Dilhi*. Internet Archive (Provided by Digital Library of India aka Public Library of India). https://archive.org/details/in.ernet.dli.2015.281500/mode/1up?view=theater Page- 294 and 295

Information From Various Articles On Internet

1. Akhtar, A., & Farani, M. (2018). *Religious policy of Emperor Shahjahan (1627 - 1658 AD)*. Research Gate. https://www.researchgate.net/publication/344658142_Religious_Policy_of_Emperor_Shahjahan_1627-1658AD Page- 159

2. Lal, K. S. (1988). *The mughal harem*. Aditya Prakashan. Page- 140, 141 and 142

3. Lal, K. S. (1988). *The mughal harem*. Aditya Prakashan. Page- 141

Bibliography

4. Akhtar, A., & Farani, M. (2018). *Religious policy of Emperor Shahjahan (1627 - 1658AD).* Research Gate. https://www.researchgate.net/publication/344658142_Religious_Policy_of_Emperor_Shahjahan_1627-1658AD Page- 163

5. Sunidhi T. (n.d.). *Religious policy of the mughal emperors/ indian history.* History Discussion. https://www.historydiscussion.net/history-of-india/mughal-emperors/religious-policy-of-the-mughal-emperors-indian-history/6620

6. Srivastava, A. L. (1986). *The mughul empire* (8th ed.). Shiva Lal Agarwala & Company. Page- 300 and 326 First edition published- 1952

7. Sunidhi T. (n.d.). *Reign of Shah Jahan: Golden age of the mughal empire/ indian history.* History Discussion. https://www.historydiscussion.net/history-of-india/shah-jahan/reign-of-shah-jahan-golden-age-of-the-mughul-empire-indian-history/6607

Golden Age of the Mughal Empire

1. Smith, V. A. (1921). *The oxford student's history of India* (9th ed.). Internet Archive (Provided by University of Toronto). https://archive.org/details/oxfordstudentshi00smituoft/Page/151/mode/1up?view=theater Page- 181

2. Sunidhi T. (n.d.). *Religious policy of the mughal emperors/ indian history.* History Discussion. https://www.historydiscussion.net/history-of-india/mughal-emperors/religious-policy-of-the-mughal-emperors-indian-history/6620

3. Sunidhi T. (n.d.). *Religious policy of the mughal emperors/ indian history.* History Discussion. https://www.historydiscussion.net/history-of-india/mughal-emperors/religious-policy-of-the-mughal-emperors-indian-history/6620

4. Smith, V. A. (1921). *The oxford student's history of India* (9th ed.). Internet Archive (Provided by University of Toronto).

https://archive.org/details/oxfordstudentshi00smituoft/Page/151/mode/1up?view=theater Page- 18

5. Srivastava, A. L. (1986). *The mughul empire* (8th ed.). Shiva Lal Agarwala & Company. Page- 324 First edition published- 1952

Chapter 6- WAR CRIMES, CRIMES AGAINST HUMANITY, AND GENOCIDE

1. United Nations Office on Genocide Prevention and the Responsibility to Protect. (n.d.). *Definitions: War Crimes.* United Nations Organisation. https://www.un.org/en/genocideprevention/war-crimes.shtml

2. United Nations Office on Genocide Prevention and the Responsibility to Protect. (n.d.). *Definitions: Crimes against humanity* . United Nations Organisation. https://www.un.org/en/genocideprevention/crimes-against-humanity.shtml

3. United Nations Office on Genocide Prevention and the Responsibility to Protect. (n.d.). *Definitions: Genocide.* United Nations Organisation. https://www.un.org/en/genocideprevention/genocide.shtml

4. International Court of Justice. (2022, December 4). In *Wikipedia.* https://en.wikipedia.org/wiki/International_Court_of_Justice#:~:text=As%20stated%20in%20Article%2093,parties%20to%20the%20court's%20statute.

5. Munjal, D. (2022, March 3). Explained | The International Criminal Court and the cases it deals with. *The Hindu.* https://www.thehindu.com/news/international/explained-the-international-criminal-court-and-the-cases-it-deals-with/article65183057.ece

Chapter 7- SIX FUNDAMENTAL RIGHTS

1. McGill University Official Site. (n.d.). *Fundamental rights in India.* cs.mcgill.ca (Provided by 2007 Schools Wikipedia Selection).

https://www.cs.mcgill.ca/~rwest/wikispeedia/wpcd/wp/f/Fundamental_Rights_in_India.htm#:~:text=Article%2021%20declares%20that%20no,attempt%20thereof%2C%20is%20an%20offence

2. BYJU'S Author. (n.d.). *Fundamental rights- Articles 12-35 (part III of Indian constitution).* https://byjus.com/free-ias-prep/fundamental-rights/

3. Government of India Official Site. (n.d.). *Constitution of India.* India.gov.in. https://www.india.gov.in/my-government/constitution-india#:~:text=The%20Republic%20is%20governed%20in,force%20on%2026th%20January%2C%201950.

Chapter 8- POLITICAL INTEGRATION OF INDIA

1. Statue of Unity Official Website. (n.d.). *Statue of unity.* https://statueofunity.in/

2. Statue of Unity Official Website. (n.d.). *Statue of unity.* https://statueofunity.in/

3. Government of India Official Website. (n.d.). *States and union territories.* Know India. https://knowindia.india.gov.in/states-uts/#:~:text=There%20are%2028%20states%20and,dress%2C%20festivals%2C%20language%20etc.

Chapter 9- THE WORKERS OF THE TAJ

1. Taj Mahal Official Website. (n.d.). *Creation history.* Tajmahal.gov.in. https://www.tajmahal.gov.in/creation-history-of-taj-mahal.aspx

2. Nicoll, F. (2009). *Shah Jahan: The rise and fall of the mughal emperor.* Haus Publishing Ltd. Page- 190

3. Hassan, J. (2021, December 29). *Shah Jahan chopped off hands of workers who built taj mahal? no, viral claim is false and baseless!* The Logical India. https://thelogicalindian.com/fact-check/shahjahan-32876

4. Deccan Herald Author. (2021, December 25). *Fact check: Did Shah Jahan chop off the hands of Taj Mahal workers?* Deccan

Herald. https://www.deccanherald.com/national/fact-check-did-shah-jahan-chop-off-the-hands-of-taj-mahal-workers-1064616.html

Chapter 10- THE BUTTERFLY EFFECT

1. Edward Norton Lorenz. (2022, November 10). In *Wikipedia*. https://en.wikipedia.org/wiki/Edward_Norton_Lorenz

2. APS News Author. (2003, January). *Circa january 1961: Lorenz and the butterfly effect* (Vol. 12: Number 1)(A. Chodos, Ed.). American Physical Society. https://www.aps.org/publications/apsnews/200301/history.cfm#:~:text=Lorenz%20subsequently%20dubbed%20his%20discovery,range%20weather%20forecasting%20was%20doomed

3. Smith, V. A. (1919). *The oxford history of India: From the earliest times to the end of 1911*. Internet Archive (Provided by University of Toronto). https://archive.org/details/oxfordhistoryofi00smituoft/Page/321/mode/1up Page- 321

4. India Today Author. (2018, February 14). *Babur: The founder of the empire which ruled India for over 300 years*. India Today. https://www.indiatoday.in/education-today/gk-current-affairs/story/mughal-emperor-babur-839094-2016-12-25

5. Andrews, E. (2014, April 29). *10 things you may not know about Genghis Khan*. History. https://www.history.com/news/10-things-you-may-not-know-about-genghis-khan#:~:text=He%20was%20responsible%20for%20the,at%20somewhere%20around%2040%20million

6. Maybell, H. (2003, February 13). *Genghis Khan a prolific lover, dna data implies*. National Geographic. https://www.nationalgeographic.com/culture/article/mongolia-genghis-khan-dna#:~:text=An%20international%20group%20of%20geneticists,16%20million%20descendants%20living%20today

7. India Today Author. (2018, April 9). *Who was Timur, the infamous mughal conqueror?* India Today.

Bibliography

https://www.indiatoday.in/education-today/gk-current-affairs/story/timur-saif-kareena-tamerlane-358789-2016-12-21

8. Britannica. (2022, October 25). Timur. In *Britannica.com Encyclopedia.* Retrieved December 6, 2022, from https://www.britannica.com/biography/Timur

9. Smith, V. A. (1919). *The oxford history of India: From the earliest times to the end of 1911.* Internet Archive (Provided by University of Toronto). https://archive.org/details/oxfordhistoryofi00smituoft/Page/321/mode/1up Page- 252

AND

Grover, N. (2023, February 17). *Timur's invasion (1398 AD) - Medieval India history notes.* Prepp India. https://prepp.in/news/e-492-timurs-invasion-1398-ad-medieval-india-history-notes

10. Beveridge, A. S. (1922). *The babur-nama in english: Memoirs of Babur* (Vol. 2). Internet Archive (Provided by University of Toronto). https://archive.org/details/baburnamaiengli02babuuoft/Page/n3/mode/2up?q=delhi Page- 484 and 596

AND

Srivastava, A. L. (1986). *The mughul empire* (8th ed.). Shiva Lal Agarwala & Company.First edition published- 1952

11. Smith, V. A. (1919). *The oxford history of India: From the earliest times to the end of 1911.* Internet Archive (Provided by University of Toronto). https://archive.org/details/oxfordhistoryofi00smituoft/Page/321/mode/1up Page- 350

12. Lal, K. S. (1988). *The mughal harem.* Aditya Prakashan. Page- 143 and 144

13. Mishra, Dr S. K. (2014, May 17). *Jallaluddin: Neither 'Mohammad'nor 'Akbar'* (From International Journal of Sciences: Basic and Applied Research). Core. https://core.ac.uk/reader/249333825

14. Smith, V. A. (1919). *The oxford history of India: From the earliest times to the end of 1911*. Internet Archive (Provided by University of Toronto). https://archive.org/details/oxfordhistoryofi00smituoft/Page/321/mode/1up Page- 326

15. Nicoll, F. (2009). *Shah Jahan: The rise and fall of the mughal emperor*. Haus Publishing Ltd. Page- 36

16. Lal, K. S. (1988). *The mughal harem*. Aditya Prakashan. Page- 72 and 138

17. Habibullah, W., & Habibullah, R. S. (2020, September 9). *Prince Khusrau: A tale of denial and death*. Live History India. https://www.livehistoryindia.com/story/eras/prince-khusrau

18. Smith, V. A. (1919). *The oxford history of India: From the earliest times to the end of 1911*. Internet Archive (Provided by University of Toronto). https://archive.org/details/oxfordhistoryofi00smituoft/Page/321/mode/1up Page- 375

19. Lal, K. S. (1988). *The mughal harem*. Aditya Prakashan. Page- 88, Point 71

20. Nicoll, F. (2009). *Shah Jahan: The rise and fall of the mughal emperor*. Haus Publishing Ltd. Page- 119

21. Nicoll, F. (2009). *Shah Jahan: The rise and fall of the mughal emperor*. Haus Publishing Ltd. Page- x and 155

22. Nicoll, F. (2009). *Shah Jahan: The rise and fall of the mughal emperor*. Haus Publishing Ltd. Page- 127

23. Nicoll, F. (2009). *Shah Jahan: The rise and fall of the mughal emperor*. Haus Publishing Ltd. Page- 257

24. Sarkar, J. (1912). *History of aurangzib: Mainly based on persian sources* (Vol. 2: War of Succession). Internet Archive (Provided by Digital Library of India aka Public Library of India). https://archive.org/details/in.ernet.dli.2015.23814/Page/n2/mode/1up?view=theater

Bibliography

25. Smith, V. A. (1919). *The oxford history of India: From the earliest times to the end of 1911.* Internet Archive (Provided by University of Toronto). https://archive.org/details/oxfordhistoryofi00smituoft/Page/321/mode/1up Page- 415, 468

26. Sarkar, J. (1912). *History of aurangzib: Mainly based on persian sources* (Vol. 2: War of Succession). Internet Archive (Provided by Digital Library of India aka Public Library of India). https://archive.org/details/in.ernet.dli.2015.23814/Page/n2/mode/1up?view=theater Page- 99, 100, 214, 217, 218 and 219

27. Sarkar, J. (1912). *History of aurangzib: Mainly based on persian sources* (Vol. 2: War of Succession). Internet Archive (Provided by Digital Library of India aka Public Library of India). https://archive.org/details/in.ernet.dli.2015.23814/Page/n2/mode/1up?view=theater Page- 236

28. Nicoll, F. (2009). *Shah Jahan: The rise and fall of the mughal emperor.* Haus Publishing Ltd. Page- 240 and 246

29. Smith, V. A. (1921). *The oxford student's history of India* (9th ed.). Internet Archive (Provided by University of Toronto). https://archive.org/details/oxfordstudentshi00smituoft/Page/151/mode/1up?view=theater Page- 207

30. Mcgee, R. (2016). *The Shah Jahan handbook- Everything you need to know about Shah Jahan.* Emereo Publishing. https://www.kobo.com/ca/en/ebook/the-shah-jahan-handbook-everything-you-need-to-know-about-shah-jahan Page- 57

31. Britannica. (n.d.). Guru Gobind Singh. In *Britannica.com Encyclopedia.* Retrieved December 7, 2022, from https://www.britannica.com/biography/Guru-Gobind-Singh

32. Bandyopadhyay, S. (2018, February 1). Militarization of the sikh panth; a classic example of devotion and dissent. *International Journal of Creative Research Thoughts, (6)1,* 419-423. https://www.ijcrt.org/papers/IJCRT1133670.pdf

33. Sikhi Wiki. (2021, August 22). Guru Tegh Bahadur. In *Sikhi Wiki Encyclopedia*. Retrieved December 7, 2022, from https://www.sikhiwiki.org/index.php/Guru_Tegh_Bahadur

34. McLeod, W. H. (2022, November 9). *Sikhism*. Britannica.com Encyclopedia. Retrieved December 8, 2022, from https://www.britannica.com/topic/Sikhism/Guru-Nanak

35. Deol, T. (2019, October 7). *Zafarnama, the 'victory letter' that Guru Gobind Singh wrote to Aurangzeb*. The Print. https://theprint.in/theprint-profile/zafarnama-victory-letter-guru-gobind-singh-wrote-aurangzeb/301792/

36. Sikhi Wiki. (2019, October 26). Zafarnama. In *Sikhi Wiki Encyclopedia*. Retrieved December 8, 2022, from https://www.sikhiwiki.org/index.php/Zafarnama

37. Sikhi Wiki. (2015, November 14). Zafarnama (english translation). In *Sikhi Wiki Encyclopedia*. Retrieved December 8, 2022, from https://www.sikhiwiki.org/index.php/Zafarnama_(English_translation)

38. Sikhi Wiki. (2019, October 26). Zafarnama. In *Sikhi Wiki Encyclopedia*. Retrieved December 8, 2022, from https://www.sikhiwiki.org/index.php/Zafarnama

39. Smith, V. A. (1919). *The oxford history of India: From the earliest times to the end of 1911*. Internet Archive (Provided by University of Toronto). https://archive.org/details/oxfordhistoryofi00smituoft/Page/321/mode/1up Page- 448

40. Shivaji. (2022, December 5). In *Wikipedia*. https://en.wikipedia.org/wiki/Shivaji

41. Smith, V. A. (1919). *The oxford history of India: From the earliest times to the end of 1911*. Internet Archive (Provided by University of Toronto). https://archive.org/details/oxfordhistoryofi00smituoft/Page/321/mode/1up Page- 469

Bibliography

42. Smith, V. A. (1921). *The oxford student's history of India* (9th ed.). Internet Archive (Provided by University of Toronto). https://archive.org/details/oxfordstudentshi00smituoft/Page/151/mode/1up?view=theater Page- 212

43. Dalrymple, W. (2015, June 22). *The great divide: The violent legacy of indian partition*. The New Yorker. https://www.newyorker.com/magazine/2015/06/29/the-great-divide-books-dalrymple

44. Google. (n.d.). Polygamy. *In Google Dictionary (Provided by Oxford Languages)*. Retrieved December 10, 2022, from https://www.google.com/search?q=polygamy+definition&rlz=1CAEVJI_enCA903CA903&oq=polyga&aqs=chrome.0.69i59j69i57j35i39j0i433i512l4j0i512j0i131i433i512j0i512.2761j1j15&sourceid=chrome&ie=UTF-8

45. Pandey, G. (2022, May 10). Polygamy: Muslim women in India fight 'abhorrent' practice. *BBC News*. https://www.bbc.com/news/world-asia-india-61351784

46. Google. (n.d.). Polygyny. *In Google Dictionary (Provided by Oxford Languages)*. Retrieved December 10, 2022, from https://www.google.com/search?q=polygyny+definition&rlz=1CAEVJI_enCA903CA903&sxsrf=ALiCzsbw0bOqjgUiBiz8P9iVNyKiOzbwKw%3A1670726867935&ei=00SVY4jYOJqI0PEP_uOIOA&ved=0ahUKEwjIjevLxvD7AhUaBDQIHf4xAgcQ4dUDCA8&uact=5&oq=polygyny+definition&gs_lcp=Cgxnd3Mtd2l6LXNlcnAQAzIFCAAQgAQyBQgAEIAEMgUIABCABDIFCAAQgAQyBQgAEIAEMgYIABAWEB4yBggAEBYQHjIICAAQFhAeEA8yCAgAEBYQHhAPMggIABAWEB4QDzoHCCMQsAMQJzoKCAAQRxDWBBCwAzoHCAAQsAMQQzoNCAAQ5AIQ1gQQsAMYATOoPCC4Q1AIQyAMQsAMQQxgCOgQIIxAnOgsIABCxAxCDARCRAjoFCAAQsQM6CwgAEIAEELEDEIMBOgUIABCRAjoECAAQAzoJCAAQCgoFQ9AVYxxhgwhtoAXABeACAAbsBiAGSDJIBBDAuMTGYAQCgAQHIARAHAAQHaAQYIARABGAnaAQYIAhABGAg&sclient=gws-wiz-serp#dobs=polygyny

47. Pandey, G. (2022, May 10). Polygamy: Muslim women in India fight 'abhorrent' practice. *BBC News*. https://www.bbc.com/news/world-asia-india-61351784

48. Nagarajan, R. (2022, July 28). Multiple wives most common among tribals: NFHS data. *Times of India.* https://timesofindia.indiatimes.com/india/multiple-wives-most-common-among-tribals-nfhs-data/articleshow/93174538.cms

49. Kramer, S. (2020, December 7). *Polygamy is rare around the world and mostly confined to a few regions.* Pew Research Center. https://www.pewresearch.org/fact-tank/2020/12/07/polygamy-is-rare-around-the-world-and-mostly-confined-to-a-few-regions/#:~:text=Polygamy%20is%20banned%20throughout%20much,to%20government%20administration%20of%20marriages.

50. Statista Research Department. (2022, October 13). *Number of reported rape cases in India 2005-2021.* Statista. https://www.statista.com/statistics/632493/reported-rape-cases-india/

51. Mascarenhas, A. (2022, April 29). Domestic violence cases in India increased 53% between 2001 and 2018: Study. *The Indian Express.* https://indianexpress.com/article/cities/pune/domestic-violence-cases-in-india-increased-53-between-2001-and-2018-study-7893930/

52. Sarkar, S. (2021, November 28). Survey shows 30% women across 14 states, UTs justify men beating their wives. *Hindustan Times.* https://www.hindustantimes.com/india-news/survey-shows-30-women-across-14-states-uts-justify-men-beating-their-wives-101638095695758.html

53. PTI Author. (2021, November 28). Over 30% women from 14 states, UT justify beating by husbands: NFHS. *Times of India.* https://timesofindia.indiatimes.com/india/over-30-women-from-14-states-ut-justify-beating-by-husbands-nfhs/articleshow/87961478.cms?utm_source=contentofinterest&utm_medium=text&utm_campaign=cppst

54. Nicoll, F. (2009). *Shah Jahan: The rise and fall of the mughal emperor.* Haus Publishing Ltd. Page- 36

Bibliography

OR

Smith, V. A. (1919). *The oxford history of India: From the earliest times to the end of 1911*. Internet Archive (Provided by University of Toronto). https://archive.org/details/oxfordhistoryofi00smituoft/Page/321/mode/1up Page- 383

55. Lal, K. S. (1988). *The mughal harem*. Aditya Prakashan. Page- 72, 174 and 175

56. Saksena, B. P. (1932). *History of Shah Jahan of Dilhi*. Internet Archive (Provided by Digital Library of India aka Public Library of India). https://archive.org/details/in.ernet.dli.2015.281500/mode/1up?view=theater Page- 18

57. Sarkar, J. (1919). *Studies in mughal India*. Internet Archive (Provided by University of Toronto). https://archive.org/details/studiesinmughali00sarkuoft/mode/1up Page- 37

58. Lal, K. S. (1988). *The mughal harem*. Aditya Prakashan. Page- 174

59. Smith, V. A. (1921). *The oxford student's history of India* (9th ed.). Internet Archive (Provided by University of Toronto). https://archive.org/details/oxfordstudentshi00smituoft/Page/151/mode/1up?view=theater Page- 186 and 187

60. Smith, V. A. (1919). *The oxford history of India: From the earliest times to the end of 1911*. Internet Archive (Provided by University of Toronto). https://archive.org/details/oxfordhistoryofi00smituoft/Page/321/mode/1up Page- 360

61. Smith, V. A. (1919). *The oxford history of India: From the earliest times to the end of 1911*. Internet Archive (Provided by University of Toronto). https://archive.org/details/oxfordhistoryofi00smituoft/Page/321/mode/1up Page- 378

62. Lal, K. S. (1988). *The mughal harem.* Aditya Prakashan. Page- 111

63. Smith, V. A. (1921). *The oxford student's history of India* (9th ed.). Internet Archive (Provided by University of Toronto). https://archive.org/details/oxfordstudentshi00smituoft/Page/151/mode/1up?view=theater Page- 204

64. Smith, V. A. (1919). *The oxford history of India: From the earliest times to the end of 1911.* Internet Archive (Provided by University of Toronto). https://archive.org/details/oxfordhistoryofi00smituoft/Page/321/mode/1up Page- 406

AND

Nicoll, F. (2009). *Shah Jahan: The rise and fall of the mughal emperor.* Haus Publishing Ltd. Page- 218 and 219

AND

Saksena, B. P. (1932). *History of Shah Jahan of Dilhi.* Internet Archive (Provided by Digital Library of India aka Public Library of India). https://archive.org/details/in.ernet.dli.2015.281500/mode/1up?view=theater Page- 176

65. Smith, V. A. (1919). *The oxford history of India: From the earliest times to the end of 1911.* Internet Archive (Provided by University of Toronto). https://archive.org/details/oxfordhistoryofi00smituoft/Page/321/mode/1up Page- 412

66. Deol, T. (2019, October 7). *Zafarnama, the 'victory letter' that Guru Gobind Singh wrote to Aurangzeb.* The Print. https://theprint.in/theprint-profile/zafarnama-victory-letter-guru-gobind-singh-wrote-aurangzeb/301792/

67. Smith, V. A. (1921). *The oxford student's history of India* (9th ed.). Internet Archive (Provided by University of Toronto). https://archive.org/details/oxfordstudentshi00smituoft/Page/151/mode/1up?view=theater Page- 207

AND

Saksena, B. P. (1932). *History of Shah Jahan of Dilhi.* Internet Archive (Provided by Digital Library of India aka Public Library of India). https://archive.org/details/in.ernet.dli.2015.281500/mode/1up?view=theater Page- 174

AND

Srivastava, A. L. (1986). *The mughul empire* (8th ed.). Shiva Lal Agarwala & Company. Page- 326 First edition published- 1952

68. Saksena, B. P. (1932). *History of Shah Jahan of Dilhi.* Internet Archive (Provided by Digital Library of India aka Public Library of India). https://archive.org/details/in.ernet.dli.2015.281500/mode/1up?view=theater Page- 18

69. Nicoll, F. (2009). *Shah Jahan: The rise and fall of the mughal emperor.* Haus Publishing Ltd. Page- 115

70. Transparency International. (2021). *Corruption perceptions index: India.* Transparency Organisation. https://www.transparency.org/en/cpi/2021/index/ind

71. Smith, V. A. (1921). *The oxford student's history of India* (9th ed.). Internet Archive (Provided by University of Toronto). https://archive.org/details/oxfordstudentshi00smituoft/Page/151/mode/1up?view=theater Page- 184

72. Sarkar, J. (1912). *History of aurangzib: Mainly based on persian sources* (Vol. 1: Reign of Shah Jahan). Internet Archive (Provided by Digital Library of India aka Public Library of India and National Archives of India). https://archive.org/details/dli.granth.88707/mode/1up Page- 180

73. Srivastava, A. L. (1986). *The mughul empire* (8th ed.). Shiva Lal Agarwala & Company. Page- 316 and 326 First edition published- 1952

74. Nicoll, F. (2009). *Shah Jahan: The rise and fall of the mughal emperor.* Haus Publishing Ltd. Page- 55

Chapter 11- CONCLUSION

1. Saksena, B. P. (1932). *History of Shah Jahan of Dilhi*. Internet Archive (Provided by Digital Library of India aka Public Library of India). https://archive.org/details/in.ernet.dli.2015.281500/mode/1up?view=theater Page- 90

2. Smith, V. A. (1919). *The oxford history of India: From the earliest times to the end of 1911*. Internet Archive (Provided by University of Toronto). https://archive.org/details/oxfordhistoryofi00smituoft/Page/321/mode/1up Page- 448

3. Nicoll, F. (2009). *Shah Jahan: The rise and fall of the mughal emperor*. Haus Publishing Ltd. Page- 196

4. Nicoll, F. (2009). *Shah Jahan: The rise and fall of the mughal emperor*. Haus Publishing Ltd. Page- 197

5. Nicoll, F. (2009). *Shah Jahan: The rise and fall of the mughal emperor*. Haus Publishing Ltd. Page 196

6. Shah Jahan. (2022, December 4). In *Wikipedia*. https://en.wikipedia.org/wiki/Shah_Jahan#:~:text=Shah%20Jahan%2C%20meaning%20%22King%20of,Timurid%20roots%20and%20his%20ambitions

7. Jahangir(name). (2022, September 11). In *Wikipedia*. https://en.wikipedia.org/wiki/Jahangir_(name)#:~:text=Jahangir%20or%20Jangir%20

8. Family Education Author. (n.d.). *Meaning and origin of: Akbar*. Family Education. https://www.familyeducation.com/baby-names/name-meaning/akbar#:~:text=Meaning%20and%20Origin%20of%3A%20Akbar&text=Muslim%20

9. She Knowns Author. (n.d.). *Alamgir*. She Knows. https://www.sheknows.com/baby-names/name/alamgir/

10. Nicoll, F. (2009). *Shah Jahan: The rise and fall of the mughal emperor*. Haus Publishing Ltd. Page- 248

Bibliography

11. Nicoll, F. (2009). *Shah Jahan: The rise and fall of the mughal emperor.* Haus Publishing Ltd. Page- 185

12. Sarkar, J. (1919). *Studies in mughal India.* Internet Archive (Provided by University of Toronto). https://archive.org/details/studiesinmughali00sarkuoft/mode/1up Page- 10

13. Smith, V. A. (1919). *The oxford history of India: From the earliest times to the end of 1911.* Internet Archive (Provided by University of Toronto). https://archive.org/details/oxfordhistoryofi00smituoft/Page/321/mode/1up Page- 409

14. Nicoll, F. (2009). *Shah Jahan: The rise and fall of the mughal emperor.* Haus Publishing Ltd. Page- 235

15. Srivastava, A. L. (1986). *The mughul empire* (8th ed.). Shiva Lal Agarwala & Company. Page- 316 First edition published- 1952

Chapter 12- ACTION

1. Taj Mahal Official Website. (n.d.). *Views of Taj Mahal.* Tajmahal.gov.in. https://www.tajmahal.gov.in/views-of-majmahal.aspx#:~:text=Taj%20Visitors,of%20October%2C%20November%20and%20February.

2. Smith, V. A. (1919). *The oxford history of India: From the earliest times to the end of 1911.* Internet Archive (Provided by University of Toronto). https://archive.org/details/oxfordhistoryofi00smituoft/Page/321/mode/1up Page- 393 and 394

3. Smith, V. A. (1919). *The oxford history of India: From the earliest times to the end of 1911.* Internet Archive (Provided by University of Toronto). https://archive.org/details/oxfordhistoryofi00smituoft/Page/321/mode/1up Page- 418

4. Sunidhi T. (n.d.). *Reign of Shah Jahan: Golden age of the mughal empire| Indian history.* History Discussion. https://www.historydiscussion.net/history-of-india/shah-

jahan/reign-of-shah-jahan-golden-age-of-the-mughul-empire-indian-history/6607

5. Anjum, F. (2007, January). *European travel writing and western perception of indo-muslim civilization in india in the seventeenth century.* Research Gate. https://www.researchgate.net/publication/317012418_European_Travel_Writing_and_Western_Perception_of_Indo-Muslim_Civilization_in_India_in_the_Seventeenth_Century Page- 117 and 121

6. Sarkar, J. (1919). *Studies in mughal India.* Internet Archive (Provided by University of Toronto). https://archive.org/details/studiesinmughali00sarkuoft/mode/1up Page- 1 and 2

7. Saksena, B. P. (1932). *History of Shah Jahan of Dilhi.* Internet Archive (Provided by Digital Library of India aka Public Library of India). https://archive.org/details/in.ernet.dli.2015.281500/mode/1up?view=theater Page- x x to x x x

8. Lal, K. S. (1988). *The mughal harem.* Aditya Prakashan. Page- 6 and 13

9. History.com Editors. (2017, October 12). *Buddhism.* History. https://www.history.com/topics/religion/buddhism

10. The Hindu Author. (2015, August 28). Delhi's Aurangzeb road renamed after Adul Kalam. *The Hindu.* https://www.thehindu.com/news/cities/Delhi/delhis-aurangzeb-road-renamed-after-abdul-kalam/article7591236.ece

For Reference Guidelines- Purdue Online Writing Lab. (n.d.). *APA formatting and style guide (7th edition).* Purdue Online Writing Lab. https://owl.purdue.edu/owl/research_and_citation/apa_style/apa_formatting_and_style_guide/index.html

THE WRITE ORDER

You Write. We Publish.

To publish your own book, contact us.

We publish poetry collections, short story collections, novellas and novels.

contact@thewriteorder.com

Instagram- thewriteorder

www.facebook.com/thewriteorder

www.ingramcontent.com/pod-product-compliance
Lightning Source LLC
LaVergne TN
LVHW010325070526
838199LV00065B/5653